Stephen
Lambie FII

THE ALEXANDER SHAKESPEARE

General Editor

R. B. KENNEDY

A Midsummer Night's Dream

Edited by

S. M. FARROW and R. B. KENNEDY

P 55

171

PREFATORY NOTE

This series of Shakespeare's plays uses the full
Alexander text which is recommended by many
Examining Boards. By keeping in mind the fact
that the language has changed considerably in
four hundred years, as have customs, jokes, and
stage conventions, the editors have aimed at
helping the modern reader – whether English
is his mother tongue or not – to grasp the full
significance of these plays. The Notes, intended
primarily for examination candidates, are presented in a simple, direct style. The needs of
those unfamiliar with British culture have been
specially considered.

Since quiet study of the printed word is unlikely
to bring fully to life plays that were written
directly for the public theatre, attention has been
drawn to dramatic effects which are important in
performance. The editors see Shakespeare's plays
as living works of art which can be enjoyed today
on stage, film and television in many parts of the
world.

First Edition 1972
Second Edition 1982

© Wm. Collins Sons and Co. Ltd.

ISBN 0 00 325247 7
Made and printed in Great Britain by
Wm. Collins and Co. Ltd., Glasgow

1 2 3 4 5 6 7 8 9

Contents

An Elizabethan playhouse. Note the apron stage protruding into the auditorium, the space below it, the inner room at the rear of the stage, the gallery above the inner stage, the canopy over the main stage, and the absence of a roof over the audience.

THE THEATRE IN SHAKESPEARE'S DAY

On the face of it, the conditions in the Elizabethan theatre were not such as to encourage great writers. The public playhouse itself was not very different from an ordinary inn-yard; it was open to the weather; among the spectators there were often louts, pickpockets and prostitutes; some of the actors played up to the rowdy elements in the audience by inserting their own jokes into the authors' lines, while others spoke their words loudly but unfeelingly; the presentation was often rough and noisy, with fireworks to represent storms and battles, and a table and a few chairs to represent a tavern; there were no actresses, so boys took the parts of women, even such subtle and mature ones as Cleopatra and Lady Macbeth; there was rarely any scenery at all in the modern sense. In fact, a quick inspection of the English theatre in the reign of Elizabeth I by a time-traveller from the twentieth century might well produce only one positive reaction: the costumes were often elaborate and beautiful.

Shakespeare himself makes frequent comments in his plays about the limitations of the playhouse and the actors of his time, often apologizing for them. At the beginning of *Henry V* the Prologue refers to the stage as 'this unworthy scaffold' and to the theatre building (the Globe, probably) as 'this wooden O', and emphasizes the urgent need for imagination in making up for all the deficiencies of presentation. In introducing Act IV the Chorus goes so far as to say:

> '. . . we shall much disgrace
> With four or five most vile and ragged foils,
> Right ill-dispos'd in brawl ridiculous,
> The name of Agincourt.' (lines 49–52)

In *A Midsummer Night's Dream* (Act V, Scene i) he seems to dismiss actors with the words:

> 'The best in this kind are but shadows.'

1

Yet Elizabeth's theatre, with all its faults, stimulated drama-
tists to a variety of achievement that has never been equalled
and, in Shakespeare, produced one of the greatest writers
in history. In spite of all his grumbles he seems to have been
fascinated by the challenge that it presented him with. It is
necessary to re-examine his theatre carefully in order to
understand how he was able to achieve so much with the
materials he chose to use. What sort of place was the
Elizabethan playhouse in reality? What sort of people were
these criticized actors? And what sort of audiences gave
them their living?

The Development of the Theatre
up to Shakespeare's Time

For centuries in England noblemen had employed groups
of skilled people to entertain them when required. Under
Tudor rule, as England became more secure and united,
actors such as these were given more freedom, and they
often performed in public, while still acknowledging their
'overlords' (in the 1570s, for example, when Shakespeare
was still a schoolboy at Stratford, one famous company was
called 'Lord Leicester's Men'). London was rapidly be-
coming larger and more important in the second half of the
sixteenth century, and many of the companies of actors
took the opportunities offered to establish themselves at
inns on the main roads leading to the City (for example, the
Boar's Head in Whitechapel and the Tabard in Southwark)
or in the City itself. These groups of actors would come to an
agreement with the inn-keeper which would give them the
use of the yard for their performances after people had
eaten and drunk well in the middle of the day. Before long,
some inns were taken over completely by companies of
players and thus became the first public theatres. In 1574
the officials of the City of London issued an order which
shows clearly that these theatres were both popular and also
offensive to some respectable people, because the order
complains about 'the inordinate haunting of great multi-
tudes of people, specially youth, to plays, interludes and
shows; namely occasion of frays and quarrels, evil practices

of incontinency in great inns . . .' There is evidence that, on public holidays, the theatres on the banks of the Thames were crowded with noisy apprentices and tradesmen, but it would be wrong to think that audiences were always un-discriminating and loud-mouthed. In spite of the disapproval of Puritans and the more staid members of society, by the 1590s, when Shakespeare's plays were beginning to be per-formed, audiences consisted of a good cross-section of English society, nobility as well as workers, intellectuals as well as simple people out for a laugh; also (and in this respect English theatres were unique in Europe), it was quite normal for respectable women to attend plays. So Shakespeare had to write plays which would appeal to people of widely different kinds. He had to provide 'some-thing for everyone' but at the same time to take care to unify the material so that it would not seem to fall into separate pieces as they watched it. A speech like that of the drunken porter in *Macbeth* could provide the 'groundlings' with a belly-laugh, but also held a deeper significance for those who could appreciate it. The audience he wrote for was one of a number of apparent drawbacks which Shakespeare was able to turn to his and our advantage.

Shakespeare's Actors

Nor were all the actors of the time mere 'rogues, vagabonds and sturdy beggars' as some were described in a Statute of 1572. It is true that many of them had a hard life and earned very little money, but leading actors could become partners in the ownership of the theatres in which they acted: Shakespeare was a shareholder in the Globe and the Black-friars theatres when he was an actor as well as a playwright. In any case, the attacks made on Elizabethan actors were usually directed at their morals and not at their acting ability; it is clear that many of them must have been good at their trade if they were able to interpret complex works like the great tragedies in such a way as to attract enthusiastic audiences. Undoubtedly some of the boys took the women's parts with skill and confidence, since a man called Coryate, visiting Venice in 1611, expressed surprise that women could act as well as they: 'I saw women act, a thing that I never saw before . . . and they performed it with as good a grace, action, gesture . . . as ever I saw any masculine actor.' The quality of most of the actors who first presented Shakespeare's plays is probably accurately summed up by Fynes Moryson, who wrote, '. . . as there be, in my opinion, more plays in London than in all the parts of the world I have seen, so do these players or comedians excel all other in the world.'

The Structure of the Public Theatre

Although the 'purpose-built' theatres were based on the inn-yards which had been used for play-acting, most of them were circular. The walls contained galleries on three storeys from which the wealthier patrons watched; they must have been something like the 'boxes' in a modern theatre, except that they held much larger numbers – as many as 1500. The 'groundlings' stood on the floor of the building, facing a raised stage which projected from the 'stage-wall', the main features of which were:

1. a small room opening on to the back of the main stage and on the same level as it (rear stage);
2. a gallery above this inner stage (upper stage);
3. a canopy projecting from above the gallery over the main stage, to protect the actors from the weather (the 700 or 800 members of the audience who occupied the yard, or 'pit' as we call it today, had the sky above them).

In addition to these features there were dressing-rooms behind the stage and a space underneath it from which entrances could be made through trap-doors. All the acting areas – main stage, rear stage, upper stage and under stage – could be entered by actors directly from their dressing-rooms, and all of them were used in productions of Shakespeare's plays. For example, the inner stage, an almost cave-like structure, would have been where Ferdinand and Miranda are 'discovered' playing chess in the last act of *The Tempest*, while the upper stage was certainly the balcony from which Romeo climbs down in Act III of *Romeo and Juliet*.

It can be seen that such a building, simple but adaptable, was not really unsuited to the presentation of plays like Shakespeare's. On the contrary, its simplicity guaranteed the minimum of distraction, while its shape and construction must have produced a sense of involvement on the part of the audience that modern producers would envy.

Other Resources of the Elizabethan Theatre

Although there were few attempts at scenery in the public theatre (painted backcloths were occasionally used in court performances), Shakespeare and his fellow playwrights were able to make use of a fair variety of 'properties'; lists of such articles have survived: they include beds, tables, thrones, and also trees, walls, a gallows, a Trojan horse and a 'Mouth of Hell'; in a list of properties belonging to the manager, Philip Henslowe, the curious item 'two mossy banks' appears. Possibly one of them was used for the

> 'bank whereon the wild thyme blows,
> Where ox-lips and the nodding violet grows'

in *A Midsummer Night's Dream* (Act II, Scene i). Once again, imagination must have been required of the audience.

Costumes were the one aspect of stage production in which trouble and expense were hardly ever spared to obtain a magnificent effect. Only occasionally did they attempt any historical accuracy (almost all Elizabethan productions were what we should call 'modern-dress' ones), but they were appropriate to the characters who wore them: kings were seen to be kings and beggars were similarly unmistakable. It is an odd fact that there was usually no attempt at illusion in the costuming: if a costume *looked* fine and rich it probably *was*. Indeed, some of the costumes were almost unbelievably expensive. Henslowe lent his company £19 to buy a cloak, and the Alleyn brothers, well-known actors, gave £20 for a 'black velvet cloak, with sleeves embroidered all with silver and gold, lined with black satin striped with gold'.

5

With the one exception of the costumes, the 'machinery' of the playhouse was economical and uncomplicated rather than crude and rough, as we can see from this second and more leisurely look at it. This meant that playwrights were stimulated to produce the imaginative effects that they wanted from the language that they used. In the case of a really great writer like Shakespeare, when he had learned his trade in the theatre as an actor, it seems that he received quite enough assistance of a mechanical and structural kind without having irksome restrictions and conventions imposed on him; it is interesting to try to guess what he would have done with the highly complex apparatus of a modern television studio. We can see when we look back to his time that he used his instrument, the Elizabethan theatre, to the full, but placed his ultimate reliance on the communication between his imagination and that of his audience through the medium of words. It is, above all, his rich and wonderful use of language that must have made play-going at that time a memorable experience for people of widely different kinds. Fortunately, the deep satisfaction of appreciating and enjoying Shakespeare's work can be ours also, if we are willing to overcome the language difficulty produced by the passing of time.

SHAKESPEARE'S LIFE AND TIMES

Very little indeed is known about Shakespeare's private life: the facts included here are almost the only indisputable ones. The dates of Shakespeare's plays are those on which they were first produced.

*   *   *

1558 Queen Elizabeth crowned.
1561 Francis Bacon born.
1564 Christopher Marlowe born.

William Shakespeare born, April 23rd, baptized April 26th.

1566
1567 Mary, Queen of Scots, deposed.
James VI (later James I of England) crowned King of Scotland.

Shakespeare's brother, Gilbert, born.

1572 Ben Jonson born.
Lord Leicester's Company (of players) licensed; later called Lord Strange's, then the Lord Chamberlain's, and finally (under James) The King's Men.
1573 John Donne born.
1574 The Common Council of London directs that all plays and playhouses in London must be licensed.
1576 James Burbage builds the first public playhouse, The Theatre, at Shoreditch, outside the walls of the City.
1577 Francis Drake begins his voyage round the world (completed 1580).
Holinshed's *Chronicles of England, Scotland and Ireland* published (which Shakespeare later used extensively).
1582

Shakespeare married to Anne Hathaway.

7

1583 The Queen's Company founded by royal warrant.

Shakespeare's daughter, Susanna, born.

1585

Shakespeare's twins, Hamnet and Judith, born.

1586 Sir Philip Sidney, the Elizabethan ideal 'Christian knight', poet, patron, soldier, killed at Zutphen in the Low Countries.

1587 Mary, Queen of Scots, beheaded.
Marlowe's *Tamburlaine* (*Part I*) first staged.

1588 Defeat of the Spanish Armada.
Marlowe's *Tamburlaine* (*Part II*) first staged.

1589 Marlowe's *Jew of Malta* and Kyd's *Spanish Tragedy* (a 'revenge tragedy' and one of the most popular plays of Elizabethan times).

1590 Spenser's *Faerie Queene* (Books I-III) published.

1592 Marlowe's *Doctor Faustus* and *Edward II* first staged. Witchcraft trials in Scotland.
Robert Greene, a rival playwright, refers to Shakespeare as 'an upstart crow' and 'the only Shake-scene in a country'.

Titus Andronicus
Henry VI, Parts I, II and III
Richard III

1593 London theatres closed by the plague.
Christopher Marlowe killed in a Deptford tavern.

Two Gentlemen of Verona
Comedy of Errors
The Taming of the Shrew
Love's Labour's Lost

1594 Shakespeare's company becomes The Lord Chamberlain's Men.

Romeo and Juliet

1595 Raleigh's first expedition to Guiana. Last expedition of Drake and Hawkins (both died).

Richard II
A Midsummer Night's Dream

1596 Spenser's *Faerie Queene* (Books IV-VI) published. James Burbage buys rooms at Blackfriars and begins to convert them into a theatre.

King John
The Merchant of Venice
Shakespeare's son Hamnet dies. Shakespeare's father is granted a coat of arms.

1597 James Burbage dies; his son Richard, a famous actor, turns the Blackfriars Theatre into a private playhouse.

Henry IV (Part I)
Shakespeare buys and redecorates New Place at Stratford.

1598 Death of Philip II of Spain.

Henry IV (Part II)
Much Ado About Nothing

1599 Death of Edmund Spenser. The Globe Theatre completed at Bankside by Richard and Cuthbert Burbage.

Henry V
Julius Caesar
As You Like It

1600 Fortune Theatre built at Cripplegate.
East India Company founded for the extension of English trade and influence in the East.
The Children of the Chapel begin to use the hall at Blackfriars.

Merry Wives of Windsor
Troilus and Cressida

1601

Hamlet
Twelfth Night

1602 Sir Thomas Bodley's library opened at Oxford.

1603 Death of Queen Elizabeth. James I comes to the throne. Shakespeare's company becomes The King's Men. Raleigh tried, condemned and sent to the Tower.

1604 Treaty of peace with Spain.

Measure for Measure
Othello
All's Well that Ends Well

1605 The Gunpowder Plot: an attempt by a group of Catholics to blow up the Houses of Parliament.

1606 Guy Fawkes and other plotters executed.

Macbeth
King Lear

1607	Virginia, in America, colonized. A great frost in England.	*Antony and Cleopatra* *Timon of Athens* *Coriolanus* Shakespeare's daughter, Susanna, married to Dr. John Hall.
1608	The company of the Children of the Chapel Royal (who had performed at Blackfriars for ten years) is disbanded. John Milton born. Notorious pirates executed in London.	Richard Burbage leases the Blackfriars Theatre to six of his fellow actors, including Shakespeare. *Pericles, Prince of Tyre*
1609		Shakespeare's *Sonnets* published.
1610	A great drought in England.	*Cymbeline*
1611	Chapman completes his great translation of the *Iliad*, the story of Troy. Authorized Version of the Bible published.	*A Winter's Tale* *The Tempest*
1612	Webster's *The White Devil* first staged.	Shakespeare's brother, Gilbert, dies.
1613	Globe Theatre burnt down during a performance of *Henry VIII* (the firing of small cannon set fire to the thatched roof). Webster's *Duchess of Malfi* first staged.	*Henry VIII* *Two Noble Kinsmen* Shakespeare buys a house at Blackfriars.
1614	Globe Theatre rebuilt 'in far finer manner than before'.	
1616	Ben Jonson publishes his plays in one volume. Raleigh released from the Tower in order to prepare an expedition to the gold mines of Guiana.	Shakespeare's daughter, Judith, marries Thomas Quiney. Death of Shakespeare on his birthday, April 23rd.
1618	Raleigh returns to England and is executed on the charge for which he was imprisoned in 1603.	
1623	Publication of the Folio edition of Shakespeare's plays.	Death of Anne Shakespeare (née Hathaway).

10

INTRODUCTION

A Midsummer Night's Dream was probably first written for an aristocratic wedding. It must have been staged in the Great Hall of an Elizabethan mansion, to fill up the wedding evening until it was time for the bride and groom to go to bed, just like *Pyramus and Thisby* in Act V of the play itself. So it's meant first as an entertainment, both funny and romantic, in praise of marriage (and in dispraise of obstinate virginity). As part of a grand social occasion it slips in graceful compliments to the noble company. The newly married pair are meant to see themselves in the royal lovers, Theseus and Hippolyta, who head a cast of noble or royal lovers and fairies – while the low-born and ignorant Athenians are laughed at none too kindly. It's designed to appeal to and flatter a well-born and cultivated audience, with its exquisite poetry and serious ideas about love and society, passion and reason, dreaming, imagination, what is real and what is not, mingled with the gaiety and enchantment of the fairytale. But the audience don't have it all their own way – Shakespeare jeers at his fine young lovers, and the whole play is a silent challenge to the listeners to dare treat it as *Pyramus and Thisby* is – quite rightly – treated. Mainly *MND* is a pastime, an escape from ordinary life, but it could also be seen as a kind of spell against evil. In it, happiness is born out of danger, and it ends with a solemn fairy blessing on the play-marriages which also serves as good wishes for the real marriage that's being celebrated. So at the end, the play comes together with the real-life situation.

Because it's a play in honour of a wedding, the marriage of Theseus and Hippolyta is the high spot of *MND*, the knot into which the different groups of characters, their adventures, and many of the play's ideas all tie. In some ways it's a complicated play, full of confusing incidents and magical changes. It is easier to sort out what's going on when we see that the characters fall into four distinct groups, all brought together by the wedding at the end. Their movements weave together like the figures of an Elizabethan dance, creating between them all the play's variety of nobility and romance, low comedy, prose, poetry, and magic ...

Theseus and Hippolyta, the royal lovers, form the first group. He is Duke of Athens, the ancient Greek city-state that we still look back to as the source of European thought and civilization. She is Queen of the Amazons, a nation of fierce woman warriors whom Theseus was supposed to have conquered. They are ideal lovers, passionate but controlled, for they are in the right relation to one another: the man has conquered the woman and her passion and imagination are directed by his reason. Though they are eagerly in love they don't turn their backs on the world to be alone together. Theseus has his job to do as ruler of Athens, and they plan to hold their marriage as publicly as possible.

As the play begins they are looking forward to this wedding, which they celebrate at the end. They're off-stage for the whole of Acts II and III (and in some productions they're played by the same actors as Oberon and Titania, the fairy King and Queen, whom they never meet). But though they don't share in the play's adventures their love provides a kind of framework, and a standard to judge other lovers by, just as it's their wedding that ties the threads of the story together.

Next come the four young lovers. Their quarrel over who's to marry whom interrupts Theseus' and Hippolyta's love-making at the beginning of the play (Act I, Scene i, line 20). Hermia's father Egeus, a fussy, selfish old man, jealous of his authority, is forcing her to marry Demetrius instead of Lysander whom she loves. He tries to control the lovers by appealing to the Duke and the Law of Athens, but in the end gets nowhere – the lovers sort out their own affairs and Duke Theseus finally refuses to support him. Lysander and Hermia (followed by Demetrius and Helena) run away from the law and the city to the wood by night, and after their adventures there, are married along with Theseus and Hippolyta (a triple wedding).

All four lovers are possessed by romantic love so extreme that it blots out their individuality. It is hard to tell the two men apart, and though the two girls are characterized more distinctly – Hermia dark, small, fierce and brave, Helena tall, fair, plaintive and self-pitying – they have those irritatingly similar names. Of course Shakespeare means them to be all alike – he's more interested in love than in the lovers – but when in the wood they begin to swop partners it's very hard to follow what happens. We need a plan which shows them going through regular movements like dance steps. They join and break hands, set to different partners, and finally end up as they began.

(1) Before the play began, Lysander loved Hermia, Demetrius loved Helena, all four were friends.

Lysander⇄Hermia   Demetrius⇄Helena

(2) Act I Scene i: Demetrius changes to Hermia, so that Helena, still loving him, is left unloved.

Lysander⇄Hermia◄——Demetrius/◄——Helena

(3) Act II Scene ii: Puck drops the love-juice in Lysander's eyes by accident, so that he falls in love with Helena and abandons Hermia. Now both partnerships are dissolved, and the four chase each other in a ring.

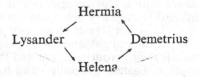

Hermia

Lysander   Demetrius

Helena

(4) Act III Scene ii: Oberon anoints Demetrius with the juice, and he wakes loving Helena. The pattern of (2) is now neatly turned round, except that Helena can't believe Demetrius loves her, and refuses him. Hermia is

left unloved, as Demetrius and Lysander quarrel over Helena. Finally they try to fight each other, and so do the two girls.

$$\text{Hermia} \longrightarrow /\text{Lysander} \longrightarrow \text{Helena} \dashleftarrow \rightarrow \text{Demetrius}$$
$$\text{Hermia/Helena} \qquad\qquad \text{Lysander/Demetrius}$$

(5) Act IV Scene i: The love-juice has been washed from Lysander's eyes; he wakes loving Hermia again. Demetrius goes on loving Helena; she accepts him. The original partners are all four friends again.

(Note: in these 'love equations' / indicates a barrier of one kind or another.)

We meet the last group of human characters in Act I Scene ii. These are the Athenian workmen, the clowns of *MND*, or as Shakespeare would have called them, the fools. They are the low comedy turn and they speak in prose. They are also amateur actors, and acting, after love, turns out to be the play's second most important subject. As loyal Athenian citizens they plan to put on a play, the tragic love-story of *Pyramus and Thisby*, for the royal wedding. While rehearsing in the wood by night, Bottom, their leading man and moving spirit, falls under enchantment and becomes the lover of the Fairy Queen, wearing a donkey's head on his human shoulders. He is disenchanted, though, in time for them to act the play on the wedding evening, so their part of the story also has a happy ending.

Then there are the fairies, Oberon and Titania (the Fairy King and Queen) and Puck. They belong to the wild wood (where the scene shifts in Act II) not to the city, and to the night, not the day, to moonlight and to magic. They are both exotic – India is their favourite haunt and they can be played with a touch of Eastern glamour – and homely and natural, specially Puck, the household and country fairy. The English country flavour contrasts strongly with the city and court atmosphere of the rest of the play. On the homely side they have a link with the workmen whom Puck despises but understands. But they are also royal. Puck is Oberon's jester and confidential servant, and Titania with her fairy attendants makes a little court for herself among the woodland flowers. Even so, they are not civilized. They belong to the fertile and abundant, mysterious and cruel natural world, and they understand lovers because the same sexual energies are at work in nature as in love. They themselves are spirits, 'shadows', and immaterial, though they can put on visible bodies if they like, and they are childless. In order to create life they seem to have to work through the physical world of nature and human beings, and so they are both drawn to and alien from humanity (as night touches yet is separate from the day).

The fairies have come to the wood near Athens to bless Theseus' and Hippolyta's marriage. But Oberon and Titania are quarrelling, and before the night is over both the young lovers and the actors too get drawn into their dispute. They must make peace and be friends again before the quarrelling lovers can be set to rights and their marriages also blessed. Oberon's and Titania's marriage is at the play's centre, as Theseus' and Hippolyta's is its goal, and the King and Queen in the wood balance the royal lovers in the city.

So the play's various adventures all end with the royal wedding. Theseus and Hippolyta have won through to harmony when the play begins – not without a fight. Their marriage promises to be perfect, and if Theseus has a 'past' (Act II, Scene i, lines 76-80) it is forgotten. The rest, the Fairy King and Queen themselves (an old married couple whose quarrel is correspondingly bitter and serious), and the young unmarried lovers, all have to go through confusion and breakdown before regaining peace, harmony, and happiness.

This process is mirrored in the play in the movement from Athens by day (Act I) to the wood at night (Acts II and III) and out again in the morning back to Athens (Act IV). The fairies, who belong to the night, still share in this struggle through darkness and danger to happiness – it's just before dawn that Oberon and Titania are reconciled. The last Act (V) happens in the Duke's palace in Athens, at night. When love is freely allowed the city is no longer hostile and restrictive, and when confusion has been overcome the night is no longer frightening; instead it's the time for happiness and love.

Since much of the play is taken up with quarrelling, more or less comic misunderstanding, and discord, the final triumphant reconciliation, love and concord are all the more satisfying. At the darkest and most hopeless hour of the night Oberon suddenly recalls the colour and light of morning, when

> . . . *the eastern gate, all fiery red,*
> *Opening on Neptune with fair blessed beams,*
> *Turns into yellow gold his salt green streams.*
>
> (Act III, Scene ii, lines 391-3)

By the end of Act IV peace is achieved, and Act V is given up to comedy, celebration, and blessing.

It's not just the people in *MND* who have to be reconciled. There are contrasts, tensions, even open war between day and night, the city and the wood, mortal and fairy, public and private life, comedy and tragedy, love and death, reason and imagination, waking and sleep or dream. The list could be longer. These conflicts are solved not so much by one side overcoming another (how can day 'overcome' night?), as by meetings and marriages between them which give birth to more complicated kinds of reality. Dancing, music, and above all happy marriage itself stand in the language of the play for these harmonious solutions.

Marriage therefore is at the heart of the play's meaning, as well as being the knot into which the strands of the story tie. But over against marriage shines the moon. The moon is changeable, indeed she passes through the same changes as the play itself. Sometimes she blesses human hopes and happiness – the new moon is a lucky fertility sign, looked forward to at the beginning and presiding over the end of the play. But when the lovers are quarrelling, and Titania falling out with Oberon, the moon is hostile, angry, chaste and cold.

One aspect of the moon, then, is her barren virginity, between which and marriage there is a debate that marriage wins. But though the moon must change to bless the marriage, the self-absorbed and wandering moon can't really be cast for a bad role in *MND*. Her cold mysterious light gives the play much of its magic. Like the night and like the fairies themselves who run beside her

> *From the presence of the sun,*
> *Following darkness like a dream . . .*
>
> (Act V, Scene i, lines 371–2)

the moon has a strange attractive power. It's the attraction of that unattainable world – forever outside our everyday down-to-earth existence, however happy, fruitful, and loving that may be – a world always beyond our reach and alien to our actual experience, that we can enter only in imagination and in dreams.

After this outline of the main elements in *A Midsummer Night's Dream*, it will be interesting to look more closely at its constituent parts, and examine the contribution each makes to the whole. Your reading of the 'Summing Up' (page 199) will benefit from a deeper understanding of the threads woven into the fabric of the play.

The Language of the Play

It isn't surprising that a play written nearly four hundred years ago should present problems of understanding to audiences nowadays. Living languages are always changing and developing, and the meaning of many words has altered considerably since Shakespeare used them. Another difficulty is that playwrights have always interested and amused audiences by making topical references. An Elizabethan audience would have instantly recognized a mention of the Armada, or something relating to the contemporary troubles in Ireland, which people in a twentieth century theatre might not notice. Although it must be said that much of what is most important 'gets across' quite readily, we can all gain more from a Shakespeare play by deepening our understanding of the text. That is why notes on the text are provided. But, however conscientiously readers follow the notes, they will only be adding to their comprehension of words and phrases. There is a broader strategy at work in Shakespeare's use of language. The style varies to suit the mood of the moment, or the personality of the speaker. *A Midsummer Night's Dream* begins with a stately, courtly conversation between Duke Theseus and his future wife:

Theseus: *Now, fair Hippolyta, our nuptial hour
Draws on apace; four happy days bring in
Another moon; but, O, methinks, how slow
This old moon wanes! She lingers my
desires . . .*

(Act I, Scene i, lines 1–4)

There is a balance and orderliness here which suits the speaker, yet there is no disguising the fact that he is a man in love, impatient to be married. When Egeus enters, with his irritable complaint about his daughter Hermia, the courtly language becomes over-emphatic, repetitive, nagging, contemptuous:

Egeus: *Thou hast by moonlight at her window
sung,
With feigning voice, verses of feigning love,
And stol'n the impression of her fantasy
With bracelets of thy hair, rings, gawds,
conceits . . .*

(Act I, Scene i, lines 30–3)

The mood has changed, and a very different personality is reflected in the words. Contrasts in language of this kind are going on all the time, sometimes from sentence to sentence, with widely varied pace and vocabulary. Look, for example, at the style of speech when the lovers are arguing in the wood, or when Bottom ponderously addresses his companions thus:

Snout: *Will not the ladies be afeard of the lion?*
Starveling: *I fear it, I promise you.*
Bottom: *Masters, you ought to consider with yourself, to bring in – God shield us! – a lion
among ladies is a most dreadful thing . . .*

(Act III, Scene i, lines 25–9)

Variety and flexibility are perhaps the most striking features of the language. It swings from noble verse to simple prose, from line-by-line back-chat to rich, extended oratory, from fairy song to the awkward melodrama of *Pyramus and Thisby*. Shakespeare's language is so fluid that there is virtually no mood or information which it cannot express. At times, indeed, the language itself seems to stand up on the stage for our attention. Listen for a moment to two passages in the last Act, when the 'mechanicals' are presenting their clumsy play:

Prologue: *We do not come, as minding to content you,*
Our true intent is. All for your delight
We are not here. That you should here repent you,
The actors are at hand; and, by their show,
You shall know all, that you are like to know.

Theseus: *This yellow doth not stand upon points.*

(Act V, Scene i, lines 113–18)

Here, poor Quince is so incompetent in his use of language that he chops up his sentences ludicrously. The response of the noble audience is to play lightly but skilfully with words in order to accentuate his clumsiness and make fun of it. The extreme contrast in word-handling is obvious, but, later in the same scene, after a good deal of the same witty contempt from the audience, sheer exasperation on the part of the actors breaks down the conventional division between them and the audience, and also between the classes. 'Moon' achieves direct communication, and evokes sympathy and a half-apology:

Moon: *All that I have to say is to tell you that the lant-horn is the moon; I, the Man i' the Moon; this thorn-bush, my thorn-bush; and this dog, my dog.*

Hippolyta: *Well shone, Moon. Truly, the moon shines with a good grace.*

(Act V, Scene i, lines 248–50, lines 257–8)

Most of the time, however, our attention is not drawn so closely to the language itself. The words normally make their effect imperceptibly, it may seem even unconsciously; and one of the most important means by which this is achieved is through imagery. The word 'imagery' covers a great range of effects, from simple, pictorial comparison, as in *the moon, like to a silver bow/New-bent in heaven,* (Act I, Scene i, lines 9–10) to a series of subtle suggestions that nudge our imagination, building up impressions and creating moods. In *A Midsummer Night's Dream* there are many references to the moon and to stars, which have a fairly obvious function in not allowing the Elizabethan audience, perhaps watching the play in broad daylight, to forget that most of the action is supposed to be taking place in a wood at night. But there is much more to these references than this practical function. We, as audience or as readers, are drawn more and more into the atmosphere of the play. It is full of pictures of Nature in England (Shakespeare makes hardly any attempt to transport us imaginatively to Ancient Greece). There are doves and nightingales, rooks and larks, red roses, hawthorn buds, wild thyme, bats, newts and blindworms – all conjuring up (there *is* a sense of magic) a detailed image of the countryside. All the characters are seen against this background.

The dominant imaginative time, within this familiar natural ambience, is that of 'glimmering night', when fantasy is given greatest scope, and when the grip of reason and orderliness is loose. This lack of rational control, in turn, is reinforced by striking and recurrent references to the changes in Nature. The movement of the seasons, and of day and night, are evidently part of such changes, but so is Nature's liability to upset and confuse, an aspect of what Shakespeare's contemporaries called 'mutability':

> . . . *we see*
> *The seasons alter: hoary-headed frosts*
> *Fall in the fresh lap of the crimson rose,*
> *And on old Hiems' thin and icy crown*
> *An odorous chaplet of sweet summer buds*
> *Is, as in mockery, set*

(Act II, Scene i, lines 106–11)

This instability, which is related directly to the temperamental variations of humanity, is reflected particularly in the changes of the moon. The lovers, all more or less 'distracted', roam the woods at night, the fairy kingdom itself is disturbed, even Bottom is 'translated' (Act III, Scene i, line 109), in more senses than one.

Yet Nature settles down again, and so does humanity. Humanity has, mysteriously, profited from the dream experience. All this is conveyed by Shakespeare's language. Words are his almost infinitely subtle instruments.

Characterization

It has often been said that Shakespeare's supreme achievement is in the depth and range of the characters he creates in his plays; that he constantly presents us with totally credible *individuals*. People sometimes come away from a good production of a Shakespeare play saying such things as 'I saw a man exactly like Fluellen at a Rugby International at Twickenham,' or 'I can really imagine meeting someone like Hamlet.' In most of his plays, certainly, the characters 'ring true'. Some of them are profound and convincing portraits of individuals, 'psychologically accurate', to use a familiar modern phrase. The author seems to have succeeded in creating *people*. He is assisted by the fact that we usually meet these characters as they are embodied by skilful actors and actresses. We watch a human being in the part, speaking the lines, frowning, moving, gesticulating. Gradually the illusion takes a grip upon us, our imaginations take over (guided by the imagination of the poet) and we react for a while as though we are watching and listening to real people living their own real lives. In *A Midsummer Night's Dream,* however, this reaction is not Shakespeare's prime intention. The main characters are acceptable enough: Theseus 'works' as Duke of Athens, and as a 'VIP' who also has a private life; there is still the vestige of a tradition about 'yokels' and 'country bumpkins' which gives us a clue to Bottom's personality; the phrase 'the generation gap' may come into our minds when we watch Egeus being the (very) heavy-handed father. But the actors and actresses usually need to 'fill out', as we say, the parts of Helena and Hermia and, particularly, Demetrius and Lysander. Shakespeare has not bothered to give very detailed information about them as individuals. And, turning to the fairies, how do we make sense of a supernatural king and queen ruling the night-time woods, let alone supposedly minute creatures called Peaseblossom, Cobweb, Moth and Mustardseed, or a mischievous magician like Puck? The only possible answer is that we must use our imaginations, as stimulated by the poet's words, accepting the characters as they relate to each other on the stage before us, and allowing them, through the words they utter, to build up for us an overall picture.

21

So 'character studies', though in some cases perfectly feasible, are not an essential exercise in studying a play like this one. We can differentiate between the people who parade before us, as Hermia and Helena were characterized earlier in this Introduction: 'Hermia dark, small, fierce and brave, Helena tall, fair, plaintive and self-pitying.' We could put together more substantial studies of some individuals, if asked to do so, building up evidence of (for example) Titania's indignation as a wronged wife, her poetic eloquence, her possessiveness towards the 'changeling boy', her determination to get her own way with Oberon, her langorous seductiveness with Bottom, and so on. Such an exercise would be pointless, however, unless it ended in an attempt to show her part in the total effect of the play. She is a representative of the world of human fantasy, and of the theme of disorder finally resolved in harmony. We should be wary of over-emphasizing the importance of characterization in *A Midsummer Night's Dream*. Here, it is a necessary ingredient of the theatrical event, and no more.

Plot

It is not very difficult to extract from this rich and complex play the story or plot upon which it is built:

Act 1 Theseus, Duke of Athens, is to marry Hippolyta, the Queen of the Amazons, whom he has conquered. He gives orders that the people of Athens should prepare to celebrate. Egeus, a prominent Athenian, brings his daughter Hermia before the Duke to insist that she should be made to marry Demetrius, not Lysander, whom she loves. The only alternatives, Egeus says, are death or lifelong seclusion in a nunnery. The Duke supports Egeus, but gives Hermia until the next new moon (that is, until the wedding-day of Theseus and Hippolyta) to make up her mind. Lysander and Hermia plan to meet in the wood outside Athens, and escape from the cruel law of the city. They carelessly reveal their plan to Hermia's friend Helena, who still loves Demetrius, although he has rejected her. Helena decides to tell Demetrius of the arrangements, knowing that he will go to the wood in pursuit of Hermia. She intends to follow him.

In the second scene of the Act, some Athenian labourers have met in a house to discuss the play they intend to present to the court on the Duke's wedding day. Bottom, a weaver, takes charge, parts are allotted, and they agree to meet in the wood to rehearse.

Act 2 The fairy creatures that inhabit the wood appear, notably Oberon and Titania (the King and Queen) and Puck, Oberon's messenger and jester. Oberon quarrels with his wife over the possession of a 'changeling boy' and all Nature is disrupted by their division. Oberon decides to squeeze the magic juice of a wild flower, Love-in-idleness, into Titania's eyes, so that she will fall madly in love with whatever creature wakes her. He hopes that the loved one will be monstrous. Demetrius and Helena enter. Demetrius intends to kill Lysander and take Hermia back to Athens; Hermia is trying to persuade Demetrius to turn to her. Oberon listens to them and afterwards orders Puck to squeeze the flower's juice into the eyes of 'a disdainful youth' from Athens, so that he will fall in love with Helena when he awakes. Oberon finds Titania asleep and drops the juice into her eyes. Puck mistakenly anoints the eyes of Lysander instead of Demetrius. Helena, still chasing Demetrius, finds Lysander asleep, fears he is injured, and awakens him. He falls wildly in love with her; she thinks he is mocking her and runs away. He follows, leaving Hermia to awaken alone and dismayed.

Act 3 The rehearsal of *Pyramus and Thisby* is proceeding near Titania's bower. Puck, for a joke, puts an ass's head on Bottom. The other workmen run away, frightened, and Bottom tries to keep his spirits up by singing loudly. He awakens Titania who falls in love with him and orders her fairy attendants to wait on him. While Puck is reporting events to Oberon, Hermia, very angry, comes on the scene pursued by

Demetrius, who, exhausted, lets her go and falls asleep. Oberon sends Puck to fetch Helena, and drops the juice into Demetrius's eyes. Helena enters, quarrelling with Lysander. Their voices wake Demetrius, who falls in love with Helena. The two men now compete for Helena's favour, as they previously did for Hermia's. Hermia returns, thinks Helena has deliberately taken Demetrius from her and becomes so angry that she threatens Helena, who runs away. The two men prepare to fight. Oberon blames Puck for the confusion and tells him to cause all four of the lovers to fall asleep near each other, and to squeeze an antidote into Lysander's eyes.

Act 4 While the four lovers sleep, Titania courts Bottom lovingly. He is now enjoying himself, and soon goes to sleep in the arms of the Fairy Queen. Oberon has meanwhile taken possession of the changeling boy. He removes the spell from Titania, wakes her, and tells Puck to take the ass's head off Bottom. The sun rises and Theseus and his courtiers arrive, hunting with hounds. They wake the sleeping lovers. Egeus again demands that his daughter Hermia should be made to marry Demetrius, but that young man is now in love with Helena. The Duke is pleased at this development and invites the two young couples to share his and Hippolyta's wedding festivities. The last of the sleepers, Bottom, wakes up with a dim but wonderful memory of a 'rare vision.' He rejoins his companions and they make final preparations for their play before the Duke.

Act 5 Theseus and Hippolyta discuss the strange events of the previous night, and Hippolyta, at least, acknowledges that it all has some mysterious significance. The 'lamentable comedy' of *Pyramus and Thisby* has pride of place at the festivities. The 'upper classes' score some rather cheap points at the expense of the 'mechanicals', but the Duke and Hippolyta maintain the social balance, with a touch of compassion. Midnight strikes, the various lovers retire, and mystery and magic, in the characters of Oberon and Puck, have the last word.

The merit of such a story-telling exercise is to 'get things straight', to see how the play works minute by minute, to see what sort of structure holds together the complex organism of ideas, themes, images and emotions that make up a poetic drama. The danger, and it is a real one, is that anyone should imagine that they have grasped the meaning of the play when they have understood the workings of the plot. A skilful playwright like Shakespeare would probably pride himself on putting together a plausible plot – though there are minor faults in this one. Why, for example, is Theseus made to say, at the beginning of the play:

> Now, fair Hippolyta, our nuptial hour
> Draws on apace. Four happy days bring in
> Another moon . . .

(Act I, Scene i, lines 1–3)

when the action that follows clearly covers only *two* days? Similarly, is it convincing that Helena should tell Demetrius about the plans of Hermia and Lysander, when this seems bound to send him rushing off to the woods after her rival? Surely Shakespeare has decided that he must get all four lovers into the wood, and hasn't managed to think up a really plausible excuse for the second pair of lovers.

We are certainly entitled to question errors and omissions and, indeed, to expect a good craftsman's job at this level. We should, however, maintain a sense of priorities. If a playwright has presented important and interesting ideas, or made serious – or genuinely humorous – comments about life, so that we leave the theatre thoughtful or amused or refreshed or stimulated, then it's likely that the plot has been crafted well enough. Matters such as plot and, in this play, characterization should be kept firmly in their place. Otherwise we might be in danger of sharing the reaction of Samuel Pepys who wrote, after seeing a production of *A Midsummer Night's Dream,* 'It is the most insipid ridiculous play that ever I saw in my life.' That would be a shared misjudgment.

Dramatic Structure and the Thematic Pattern

The dramatic structure of the play is something quite different from the plot, much more subtle and much more difficult to describe. If the structure doesn't vitally depend on fully developed characterization, or on a very carefully organized plot, what does it depend on? There is a widespread belief in the need for shape and order in works of art, as the fact that *A Midsummer Night's Dream* is invariably printed in five Acts demonstrates. Yet Shakespeare himself did not split it up into these numbered chunks. The shape of the play is not as simple as this, and it doesn't depend on measurement or symmetry. The heart of the matter is in the contrast between 'Athens' and the wood, which is related to the contrast between daytime and night-time, between intellectual order and instinct. Since the play begins in the city, moves out to the wood and then returns to the city, this A-B-A shape can be regarded as the true basic structure. It should, however, be noted that the fairies make the final comment, invading the city, visiting the 'hallowed house' and blessing it in their own way. This suggests that the previously opposed elements *can* come together in (perhaps precarious) harmony.

Another way of reconciling these elements in the play might be to say that the 'Midsummer Dream' is the mid-play dream, between two episodes of human order and control presided over by the patriarchal Duke (who himself invades the alternative territory for recreation, when he goes hunting). The famous Peter Brook production of the play at Stratford in 1970 linked these themes by giving the roles of Theseus and Oberon, Hippolyta and Titania to the same actor and actress, demonstrating that the apparently opposite worlds and characters of the play are really different aspects of our human experience which need not be eternally alien to each other.

If we go a little more deeply into the basic structure described above (apparently simple, but loaded with great significance) we shall see that the Athenian scenes are essentially realistic. They present familiar human experiences, drawn from ordinary life: a ruler preparing to marry the woman of his choice, four young people struggling to sort out their relationships, a group of workmen trying to organize themselves. Then we are suddenly plunged into the moonlit woodland and shown a community of the night. The fairy who talks to Puck wanders under 'the moon's sphere', and Puck calls himself a 'wanderer of the night': the fact that they are both 'wanderers' seems quite important. Their king and queen are also rootless, drifting effortlessly from Greece to India and back again. For this is a country of the imagination not controlled by reason and, perhaps consequently, disturbed and disorderly when we first visit it. All the important human characters enter the wood. They all go through the experience of dreaming; most of them explore the shadowy moonlit realm and return from it changed by a disturbing, but not deadly, experience. This central part of the play is a departure from realism; normal values do not operate here. When the characters go back to Athens, the everyday order operates again. The 'hard-handed men' struggle with their words once more, the Duke resumes his duty as a figure of authority, the lovers prepare to 'settle down' to the routine of domestic life. But none of them will ever be quite the same again after the experience of the night in the wood, or even second-hand contact with it. In spite of his word-trouble, no-one puts it better than Bottom:

It shall be call'd 'Bottom's Dream', because it hath no bottom.

(Act IV, Scene ii, lines 214–15)

He recognizes that he has had a vital experience which he will never be able to define or describe. *Something* happened in the wood, to him and to the others. What was it, essentially? Perhaps it was an acknowledgement of something in themselves that they had never before allowed to develop. To pin it down neatly and accurately is as difficult for us as it is for Bottom.

This cluster of contrasts and apparent contradictions forms the real 'dramatic structure' of the play. The pattern may look clear-cut when presented in A-B-A terms, but the ideas that evolve cannot be expressed by mathematical formulae, because they involve the baffling complexity of human thought and emotion.

Some of the recurrent themes of the play which centre on the contrast and reconciliation of opposites are presented in the Theme Index at the end of this edition.

After having looked at separate aspects and elements of *A Midsummer Night's Dream,* it is important to consider our overall view of the play. What an audience or reader should take away is the sense of a fully integrated experience. On page 199, therefore, is a section following the end of the play in which dramatic unity is stressed. Don't be too worried if you cannot fully share the experience outlined. One of the delights of Shakespeare's plays is that every time you re-read them, every time you see a new production, there is a good chance that your perception will be further enriched and you will find deeper enjoyment.

LIST OF CHARACTERS

THESEUS, *Duke of Athens*
EGEUS, *father to Hermia*
LYSANDER ⎫
DEMETRIUS ⎭ *in love with Hermia*
PHILOSTRATE, *Master of the Revels to Theseus*
QUINCE, *a carpenter*
SNUG, *a joiner*
BOTTOM, *a weaver*
FLUTE, *a bellows-mender*
SNOUT, *a tinker*
STARVELING, *a tailor*
HIPPOLYTA, *Queen of the Amazons, betrothed to Theseus*
HERMIA, *daughter to Egeus, in love with Lysander*
HELENA, *in love with Demetrius*
OBERON, *King of the Fairies*
TITANIA, *Queen of the Fairies*
PUCK, *or* ROBIN GOODFELLOW
PEASEBLOSSOM ⎫
COBWEB ⎪
MOTH ⎬ *fairies*
MUSTARDSEED ⎭

PROLOGUE		QUINCE
PYRAMUS		BOTTOM
THISBY	*presented*	FLUTE
WALL	*by*	SNOUT
MOONSHINE		STARVELING
LION		SNUG

OTHER FAIRIES *attending their King and Queen*
ATTENDANTS *on Theseus and Hippolyta*

THE SCENE: *Athens and a wood near it*

29

NOTES

ACT ONE

1-19. These opening lines are vitally important, for they must strike the keynote of harmony, quickly lost and only regained towards the close of the play. Theseus and Hippolyta, the royal lovers, are not stiff, they are passionate and tender, but they are also dignified. Their union reconciles spontaneous love with social order, and though the day of their wedding will be filled with public ceremony and rejoicing, the night will satisfy their own strong desires. They could sweep on from opposite sides of the stage, each followed by a crowd of richly dressed attendants, meet, and kiss – just long enough to show they mean it. The pattern of movement could suggest dancing; the mood is urgent, joyful, but controlled.

1-2. *our nuptial hour Draws on apace:* 'our wedding-day's coming fast'. Theseus and Hippolyta are going to be married in four days' time, at the new moon (which the Elizabethans thought was a lucky time for weddings, promising fertility). In fact, the play's action takes under three days: the young lovers run off to the wood *tomorrow night* (Act I, Scene i, line 164) and are married along with Theseus and Hippolyta the next day. Perhaps Shakespeare confused the times when he revised the play for a fresh performance, or the longer time here in Scene i may be deliberately meant to build up suspense before getting on more quickly with the action.

4. *lingers my desires:* 'holds up the satisfaction of my desires'.

5-6. Theseus imagines the moon as a wrinkled old woman who lives on and on while the heir grows as impatient for the full enjoyment of his wealth (*revenue*) as Theseus is to enjoy Hippolyta. *Step-dame* means 'stepmother'; a *dowager* is a widow with the right to a living out of her dead husband's money.

7. *steep:* sink (as the sun sinks into the sea at night).

7-8. Hippolyta, picturing time rushing on to the wedding, is as eager as Theseus to consummate their marriage. Day and night, which are so important in the play, are first mentioned here.

9-10. In contrast to Theseus, Hippolyta has a lovely image for the fresh new moon. Herself a warrior and huntress, she thinks of the moon as a great bow. Notice how the moon and its changes, moonlight, and the moon-goddess, keep coming into the play.

11. *our solemnities:* 'our marriage ceremony'.

11-15. Theseus gives instructions to Philostrate, his master of ceremonies, that public gaiety must reflect the royal lovers' happiness.

13. *pert and nimble:* lively and active.

15. *The pale companion:* 'that dismal-looking fellow'. Theseus treats *Mirth* and *Melancholy* as real people – he doesn't want a wet blanket like *Melancholy* (unhappiness) at his party. *pomp:* splendid ceremonial.

ACT ONE

Enter THESEUS, HIPPOLYTA, PHILOSTRATE
and ATTENDANTS

Theseus
  Now, fair Hippolyta, our nuptial hour
  Draws on apace; four happy days bring in
  Another moon; but, O, methinks, how slow
  This old moon wanes! She lingers my desires,
  Like to a step-dame or a dowager,   5
  Long withering out a young man's revenue.
Hippolyta
  Four days will quickly steep themselves in night;
  Four nights will quickly dream away the time;
  And then the moon, like to a silver bow
  New-bent in heaven, shall behold the night   10
  Of our solemnities.
Theseus   Go, Philostrate,
  Stir up the Athenian youth to merriments;
  Awake the pert and nimble spirit of mirth;
  Turn melancholy forth to funerals;
  The pale companion is not for our pomp.   15
               [*Exit* PHILOSTRATE]

16. Theseus fought and mastered the Amazon queen in battle. Now he can be loving and generous for she is in the right place for an Elizabethan wife: only when the man rules the woman, his natural inferior, can marriage be happy, and in this play Theseus and Hippolyta enjoy an ideal relationship.

22. Now a quarrel breaks in on the happy opening mood. Hermia is pale and determined, old Egeus and the rival lovers so angry that even Theseus' presence barely restrains them from rudeness. Theseus probably sits in judgment with Hippolyta silent beside him. The rest all stand.

27. Notice that even Egeus, who strongly disapproves of love because it makes his daughter defy him, thinks of it as a kind of magic, and the play shows that he is right. (It seems possible that Shakespeare really wrote 'witch'd', not *bewitch'd*: certainly the extra syllable sounds awkward.)

28. *Thou, thou* . . . Egeus – who is fussy, pompous, and excitable – is spluttering with rage.

28-38. Egeus accuses Lysander of tricking Hermia into love with poems, lying (*feigning*) songs sung by *moonlight*, and gifts (*gawds . . . sweetmeats*) of trinkets, flowers and food.

32. *stol'n the impression of her fantasy:* 'secretly stamped yourself on her imagination' (as a seal is stamped in warm wax) so that Hermia can dream of no one else.

35. *prevailment:* power. *unhardened:* inexperienced. (Still soft, like wax.)

36. *filch'd:* stolen.

37-8. This is the crunch. Egeus must have Hermia's absolute obedience, and the suspicion that she has a will of her own drives him crazy with a kind of jealousy.

39. *Be it so:* if.

39-45. Egeus calls on an Athenian law which gives him, as a father, total power over his daughter: if she disobeys he can have her put to death.

45. *Immediately:* on purpose.

Hippolyta, I woo'd thee with my sword,
And won thy love doing thee injuries;
But I will wed thee in another key,
With pomp, with triumph, and with revelling.

Enter EGEUS, *and his daughter* HERMIA, LYSANDER
and DEMETRIUS

Egeus
  Happy be Theseus, our renowned Duke!   20
Theseus
  Thanks, good Egeus; what's the news with thee?
Egeus
  Full of vexation come I, with complaint
  Against my child, my daughter Hermia.
  Stand forth, Demetrius. My noble lord,
  This man hath my consent to marry her.   25
  Stand forth, Lysander. And, my gracious Duke,
  This man hath bewitch'd the bosom of my child.
  Thou, thou, Lysander, thou hast given her rhymes,
  And interchang'd love-tokens with my child;
  Thou hast by moonlight at her window sung,   30
  With feigning voice, verses of feigning love,
  And stol'n the impression of her fantasy
  With bracelets of thy hair, rings, gawds, conceits,
  Knacks, trifles, nosegays, sweetmeats—messengers
  Of strong prevailment in unhardened youth;   35
  With cunning hast thou filch'd my daughter's heart;
  Turn'd her obedience, which is due to me,
  To stubborn harshness. And, my gracious Duke,
  Be it so she will not here before your Grace
  Consent to marry with Demetrius,   40
  I beg the ancient privilege of Athens:
  As she is mine I may dispose of her;
  Which shall be either to this gentleman
  Or to her death, according to our law
  Immediately provided in that case.   45

46. *Be advis'd:* think better of it.

48. *compos'd:* put together.

46-51. Theseus, who as Duke of Athens has to uphold the law and keep the peace, urges Hermia that since her father created her he has the right to destroy her, just as he could choose to keep or break a shape he'd stamped in wax.

54. 'But as a husband, since your father doesn't approve . . .'

57. Theseus tries to persuade Hermia that since her father doesn't see it her way she must see it his.

60-1. *concern my modesty . . . thoughts:* 'be fitting for me as a modest woman to speak out like this before such an important person as the Duke'. Hermia is behaving very boldly in speaking for herself, but of course love is the power that drives her.

63. *befall me:* 'happen to me'.

65. *die the death:* be executed.

65-6. *abjure For ever the society of men:* 'swear to give up male company for ever'.

67-70. Theseus, who knows that women are not just dolls without feelings or desires, asks Hermia if she can bear to live without love. *know of:* find out from. *blood:* passions, sexuality.

69-70. *Whether . . . You can endure the livery of a nun:* 'Whether you can bear to wear nun's uniform' (that is, simply, to be a nun.)

71. *For aye:* For ever. *cloister:* convent.

71-3. Theseus makes convent life sound unpleasant and unhealthy by describing it in chilly, depressing words: *shady; mew'd* (shut up, like a bird in a cage); *barren* (childless); *faint;* and the *cold fruitless moon*. This gloomy prospect is meant to put Hermia off – but it also chimes in with the play's general praise of marriage, fertility and a full sexual life rather than one of virginity.

73. *cold fruitless moon:* Diana the moon-goddess, who is a virgin herself and served by virgins.

74-8. Though those who can control their passions so as to journey through life unmarried may win the greatest spiritual reward, Theseus thinks married women are far *earthlier happy* (happier on earth).

Theseus

What say you, Hermia? Be advis'd, fair maid.
To you your father should be as a god;
One that compos'd your beauties; yea, and one
To whom you are but as a form in wax,
By him imprinted, and within his power   50
To leave the figure, or disfigure it.
Demetrius is a worthy gentleman.

Hermia

So is Lysander.

Theseus   In himself he is;
But, in this kind, wanting your father's voice,
The other must be held the worthier.   55

Hermia

I would my father look'd but with my eyes.

Theseus

Rather your eyes must with his judgment look.

Hermia

I do entreat your Grace to pardon me.
I know not by what power I am made bold,
Nor how it may concern my modesty   60
In such a presence here to plead my thoughts;
But I beseech your Grace that I may know
The worst that may befall me in this case,
If I refuse to wed Demetrius.

Theseus

Either to die the death, or to abjure   65
For ever the society of men.
Therefore, fair Hermia, question your desires,
Know of your youth, examine well your blood,
Whether, if you yield not to your father's choice,
You can endure the livery of a nun,   70
For aye to be in shady cloister mew'd,
To live a barren sister all your life,
Chanting faint hymns to the cold fruitless moon.
Thrice-blessed they that master so their blood
To undergo such maiden pilgrimage;   75

76. *the rose distill'd:* the rose whose sweet essence has been extracted. Just as the perfume of a rose can be bottled and kept, so a married woman's youth and beauty are preserved in her children.

80. *yield my virgin patent up:* 'give up my right to stay a virgin'.
80-2. When Hermia marries she will exchange the authority of her father for that of her husband, and so she is determined to choose her own master. *Lordship* and *sovereignty* mean 'authority' and 'the right to rule', and a *yoke* (the heavy wooden bar laid across the necks of ploughing oxen) is the sign of slavery.

84-5. *sealing-day . . . fellowship:* the day on which Theseus and Hippolyta will confirm their contract as companions for life. *Fellowship* implies that they will be friends rather than master and slave (though Theseus by conquering Hippolyta has already won back man's natural place as woman's superior).

88. *as he would:* 'as your father wishes'.

89. *Diana:* the goddess of chastity whom Hermia will have to promise to serve. *protest:* promise.

92. *crazed title:* 'claim that won't hold water' (*crazed* means broken or cracked). *certain right.* Demetrius thinks her father's support gives him a right to Hermia – but Lysander, who has her love, laughs at him.

95-8. Egeus still treats Hermia as a piece of property which he means to make over to (*estate unto*) Demetrius, but the clearer it is that love's power is greater than his, the angrier he gets.
96. *render:* give.

99-110. Now Lysander speaks directly to the Duke: he is as well-born and rich as Demetrius, if not richer, and above all Hermia loves him, so why shouldn't he press his claim to her (*prosecute my right*) – specially since Demetrius has just jilted another poor girl, Helena?

But earthlier happy is the rose distill'd
Than that which withering on the virgin thorn
Grows, lives, and dies, in single blessedness.

Hermia

So will I grow, so live, so die, my lord,
Ere I will yield my virgin patent up   80
Unto his lordship, whose unwished yoke
My soul consents not to give sovereignty.

Theseus

Take time to pause; and by the next new moon—
The sealing-day betwixt my love and me
For everlasting bond of fellowship—   85
Upon that day either prepare to die
For disobedience to your father's will,
Or else to wed Demetrius, as he would,
Or on Diana's altar to protest
For aye austerity and single life.   90

Demetrius

Relent, sweet Hermia; and, Lysander, yield
Thy crazed title to my certain right.

Lysander

You have her father's love, Demetrius;
Let me have Hermia's; do you marry him.

Egeus

Scornful Lysander, true, he hath my love;   95
And what is mine my love shall render him;
And she is mine; and all my right of her
I do estate unto Demetrius.

Lysander

I am, my lord, as well deriv'd as he,
As well possess'd; my love is more than his;   100
My fortunes every way as fairly rank'd,
If not with vantage, as Demetrius';
And, which is more than all these boasts can be,
I am belov'd of beauteous Hermia.
Why should not I then prosecute my right?   105
Demetrius, I'll avouch it to his head,

110. *spotted:* stained with evil (like the spotted snake, symbol of treachery).

113. *self-affairs:* 'my own affairs'.

114-21. The Duke is in a difficulty. He has failed to persuade Hermia into obedience, and cannot set the law aside. But though Egeus and Demetrius are legally in the right they are behaving stupidly and unkindly. So he breaks the party up, and takes them aside for some (*private schooling*) advice while repeating to Hermia that she must obey her father or be punished.

117-18. *look you arm . . . will:* 'make sure you get ready to bring your desires into line with your father's purpose'.

120. *extenuate:* soften.

122. *what cheer . . . ?:* 'how are you doing?' Hippolyta has had to wait in silence throughout the whole argument.

123-7. 'Help with the wedding arrangements' may be Theseus' excuse for a private argument with Egeus and Demetrius. Followed by the attendants and with Hippolyta at his side he leads them firmly out. The unhappy lovers take care to be left behind. Though they use this unexpected time alone together to make practical plans of elopement, Lysander and Hermia are most eager to talk about love itself, which has put them at odds with their society. Their dialogue is intimate and charged with emotion – they are in love and sharing a private experience which fathers and laws don't take into account.

128. *How now . . . ?:* 'how are you?' The lovers haven't been able to speak to each other before. Hermia's father has discussed her as a thing before her face – now Lysander speaks to her directly.

129. *How chance . . . ?:* why?

130. *Belike:* perhaps.

131. *Beteem them:* give them, pour out for them. Hermia is on the verge of tears, after the strain of answering Theseus boldly and with composure. Notice the lovers' poetical way of talking, in contrast to the direct and vigorous argument of the quarrel. Being in love has lifted them out of the everyday world – and as fashionable young people they also know that elegant flowery language is proper for lovers.

132-55. The belief that true love is always troubled comforts the lovers. It cheers them to be able to square their own disturbing experience with what they've heard about love, and helps them to defy everyone they owe obedience to.

132. *aught:* anything.

135. 'But either the lovers came from different backgrounds . . .'

Made love to Nedar's daughter, Helena,
And won her soul; and she, sweet lady, dotes,
Devoutly dotes, dotes in idolatry,
Upon this spotted and inconstant man.   *110*

Theseus

I must confess that I have heard so much,
And with Demetrius thought to have spoke thereof;
But, being over-full of self-affairs,
My mind did lose it. But, Demetrius, come;
And come, Egeus; you shall go with me;   *115*
I have some private schooling for you both.
For you, fair Hermia, look you arm yourself
To fit your fancies to your father's will,
Or else the law of Athens yields you up—
Which by no means we may extenuate—   *120*
To death, or to a vow of single life.
Come, my Hippolyta; what cheer, my love?
Demetrius, and Egeus, go along;
I must employ you in some business
Against our nuptial, and confer with you   *125*
Of something nearly that concerns yourselves.

Egeus

With duty and desire we follow you.

Exeunt all but LYSANDER *and* HERMIA

Lysander

How now, my love! Why is your cheek so pale?
How chance the roses there do fade so fast?

Hermia

Belike for want of rain, which I could well   *130*
Beteem them from the tempest of my eyes.

Lysander

Ay me! for aught that I could ever read,
Could ever hear by tale or history,
The course of true love never did run smooth;
But either it was different in blood——   *135*

136. *cross:* something that gets in the way – so there's a bar to happiness when a tycoon loves a factory girl (or, in Elizabethan terms, when a lord loves a milkmaid).

137. 'Or else badly matched in age.' *Misgraffed* means 'wrongly grafted'; an image from gardening. Young and old shouldn't marry, just as it would be wrong to graft a young shoot on a very old tree.

139. *friends:* relatives, one's family. This is Hermia's misfortune, to have a husband chosen for her by her father.

141-2. 'Or, if two people do choose each other freely, some disaster attacks their love.'

143-4. These images are as short and quick as the course of love itself. *Shadow* and *dream* are both key words in *MND*.

145-9. It's because he's in love and feeling intensely alive that Lysander's so conscious of the threat of death, imagined as black night, the enemy of love, light and life itself. This vivid statement of love and death bound together in one experience stands out from the play's action – but of course Hermia's father has already threatened her with death because she is in love.

145. *collied:* blackened – as black as coal.

146. *in a spleen:* in a flash of temper. *unfolds:* lights up.

149. *quick:* quickly. *confusion:* destruction.

151. *edict in destiny:* law of fate.

152-5. If bad luck is as much a natural part of love as restlessness and longing, then Hermia is willing to put up with it.

152. *teach our trial patience:* 'be patient under our troubles'.

153. *customary:* usual.

155. *Fancy:* Romance.

156. *persuasion:* argument. Lysander agrees, but he also means to do something about their situation, and goes on to unfold his plan.

158. *Of great revenue:* very rich.

159. Her house is twenty miles from Athens. (A *league* is about three miles.)

160. *respects me:* 'looks on me'.

164. *steal forth:* sneak out of. Hermia's escape is both secret and illegal.

Hermia
  O cross! too high to be enthrall'd to low.
Lysander
  Or else misgraffed in respect of years—
Hermia
  O spite! too old to be engag'd to young.
Lysander
  Or else it stood upon the choice of friends—
Hermia
  O hell! to choose love by another's eyes.   **140**
Lysander
  Or, if there were a sympathy in choice,
  War, death, or sickness, did lay siege to it,
  Making it momentary as a sound,
  Swift as a shadow, short as any dream,
  Brief as the lightning in the collied night   **145**
  That, in a spleen, unfolds both heaven and earth,
  And ere a man hath power to say 'Behold!'
  The jaws of darkness do devour it up;
  So quick bright things come to confusion.
Hermia
  If then true lovers have been ever cross'd,   **150**
  It stands as an edict in destiny.
  Then let us teach our trial patience,
  Because it is a customary cross,
  As due to love as thoughts and dreams and sighs,
  Wishes and tears, poor Fancy's followers.   **155**
Lysander
  A good persuasion; therefore, hear me, Hermia:
  I have a widow aunt, a dowager
  Of great revenue, and she hath no child—
  From Athens is her house remote seven leagues—
  And she respects me as her only son.   **160**
  There, gentle Hermia, may I marry thee;
  And to that place the sharp Athenian law
  Cannot pursue us. If thou lovest me then,
  Steal forth thy father's house to-morrow night;

167. 'To go maying.' Elizabethans still celebrated Maytime by going out at dawn to the fields and woods. (We have almost lost the summer festivals though we keep the winter ones like Bonfire Night, Hallowe'en and Christmas itself.)

168. *stay for:* wait for.

168-78. Hermia swears by everything she can think of that stands for passionate or faithful love.

169. *Cupid:* the god of love.

170. Cupid shot people with his gold arrows to make them fall in love.

171. Venus, the goddess of love, rode in a chariot drawn by doves. *Simplicity* means wholeheartedness – doves are supposed to be very loving and faithful creatures.

173. Dido, Queen of Carthage, burnt herself to death when her lover, the Trojan hero Aeneas, sailed off to found the city of Rome.

174. *Troyan:* Trojan.

179. *Keep promise, love.* Lysander laughs gently at Hermia's earnestness. But without knowing it, at the moment of giving up home and safety for love, she's pleading with *him* to be faithful to her. Not only death ends love – another threat is lovers' own inconstancy, and so they seem to feel the need to bind themselves with vows.

180. 'Hullo, Helena, where are you going?' Helena, the fourth lover, is the girl Demetrius has jilted. She's unhappy and inclined to be jealous of Hermia.

181-2. *fair:* beautiful. 'Don't call me beautiful', she says, 'it's your beauty Demetrius loves, you lucky pretty girl' (*O happy fair!*).

183. *lode-stars:* guiding stars, like the pole-star sailors steer by. *air:* musical sound.

183-5. *your tongue's sweet air . . . appear:* 'your voice is more musical than the lark sounds to a shepherd in springtime'.

184. *tuneable:* musical. Traditionally, shepherds are themselves poets and lovers.

185. *When wheat is green:* i.e. 'In the springtime'.

186. *Sickness is catching:* the idea of illness comes readily into lovesick minds. *favour:* good looks.

188. 'My ear would catch the sound of your voice, so that I'd speak like you.'

190. *Demetrius being bated:* 'except for Demetrius' (who is all the world to her).

191. *translated:* changed into.

192-3. 'By what magic do you make Demetrius love you?'

194-201. These lines show how contradictory and unreasonable people are in love. Demetrius persists in loving the girl who hates him and hating the girl who loves him. His own feelings are so strong he takes no notice at all of theirs.

And in the wood, a league without the town,   *165*
Where I did meet thee once with Helena
To do observance to a morn of May,
There will I stay for thee.
Hermia   My good Lysander!
I swear to thee by Cupid's strongest bow,
By his best arrow, with the golden head,   *170*
By the simplicity of Venus' doves,
By that which knitteth souls and prospers loves,
And by that fire which burn'd the Carthage Queen,
When the false Troyan under sail was seen,
By all the vows that ever men have broke,   *175*
In number more than ever women spoke,
In that same place thou hast appointed me,
To-morrow truly will I meet with thee.
Lysander
Keep promise, love. Look, here comes Helena.

Enter HELENA

Hermia
God speed fair Helena! Whither away?   *180*
Helena
Call you me fair? That fair again unsay.
Demetrius loves your fair. O happy fair!
Your eyes are lode-stars and your tongue's sweet air
More tuneable than lark to shepherd's ear,
When wheat is green, when hawthorn buds appear. *185*
Sickness is catching; O, were favour so,
Yours would I catch, fair Hermia, ere I go!
My ear should catch your voice, my eye your eye,
My tongue should catch your tongue's sweet melody.
Were the world mine, Demetrius being bated,   *190*
The rest I'd give to be to you translated.
O, teach me how you look, and with what art
You sway the motion of Demetrius' heart!
Hermia
I frown upon him, yet he loves me still.

206. *graces:* powers of pleasing. Hermia was perfectly happy in Athens till she fell in love with Lysander, but now she's forbidden to love him it's like hell.

209. *Phoebe:* the moon (another name for the moon-goddess).

210. *visage:* face. *glass:* mirror. The self-admiring moon gazes by night into the still water of rivers, lakes and seas.
211. 'Adorning the blades of grass with drops of dew like pearls.' Dew was thought to fall from the moon.
212. *still:* always. (Here night is friendly to lovers.)
213. *devis'd:* planned.

215. *faint primrose beds:* beds of pale primroses – suitable beds for immature girls to lie on.
216. 'Telling each other all our secrets.'

219. *stranger companies:* strange companions. Love breaks old friendships as well as family ties.

Helena

  O that your frowns would teach my smiles such skill!   *195*

Hermia

  I give him curses, yet he gives me love.

Helena

  O that my prayers could such affection move!

Hermia

  The more I hate, the more he follows me.

Helena

  The more I love, the more he hateth me.

Hermia

  His folly, Helena, is no fault of mine.   *200*

Helena

  None, but your beauty; would that fault were mine!

Hermia

  Take comfort: he no more shall see my face;
  Lysander and myself will fly this place.
  Before the time I did Lysander see,
  Seem'd Athens as a paradise to me.   *205*
  O, then, what graces in my love do dwell,
  That he hath turn'd a heaven unto a hell!

Lysander

  Helen, to you our minds we will unfold:
  To-morrow night, when Phœbe doth behold
  Her silver visage in the wat'ry glass,   *210*
  Decking with liquid pearl the bladed grass,
  A time that lovers' flights doth still conceal,
  Through Athens' gates have we devis'd to steal.

Hermia

  And in the wood where often you and I
  Upon faint primrose beds were wont to lie,   *215*
  Emptying our bosoms of their counsel sweet,
  There my Lysander and myself shall meet;
  And thence from Athens turn away our eyes,
  To seek new friends and stranger companies.
  Farewell, sweet playfellow; pray thou for us,   *220*
  And good luck grant thee thy Demetrius!

223. *lovers' food:* i.e., the sight of one another. Lysander and Hermia, as the rich style of the last two speeches shows, are in a dreamy enchanted mood. They don't really notice how sore Helena feels, or that she can't be safely trusted with their plans.

226. 'How much happier some people can be than others.'

230-1. 'Just as Demetrius is in the wrong to be violently attracted to Hermia, so am I to admire him.' Helena knows she's a fool but she can't help it.

232-45. Helena too now draws general ideas about what love is like from her own experience. Hermia and Lysander, who are happy but persecuted, saw outside threats to love (lines 132-55): Helena, who is unhappy, sees its essential weaknesses.

232-3. 'Love can change worthless things into something that seems worthwhile.' (*holding no quantity:* whose worth in themselves has no relation to the high value set on them by love.)

234-41. Helena describes Cupid (=love). He's blindfolded because people in love can't see what the beloved is really like, he has wings because he rushes into love without stopping to think, and he's only a child because he keeps changing his mind.

237. *figure:* stand for. *unheedy:* careless.

239. *beguil'd:* deceived. He so often makes the wrong choice.

240. 'As mischievous boys break their promises in fun.'

241. *is perjur'd:* breaks promises.

242. *eyne:* eyes.

243. *hail'd down oaths:* swore fast and hard.

244-5. Helena talks as if Demetrius' words were showers of real hail that melted in the sunlight of Hermia's beauty. (Helena puns on 'hail' though she's unhappy – playing on words may be a sign of strong feelings.)

246. Love makes Helena disloyal to her friend.

248-9. 'And if Demetrius thanks me for this news (*intelligence*) that's all the reward I'll get – and even that will cost him an effort'.

250-1. But even though Demetrius is cruel to her she'll have the painful pleasure of being with him. It may seem unlikely that Helena would tell tales to Demetrius, when if only Hermia escaped he would lose her and perhaps come back to Helena herself. But for his plot's sake Shakespeare must somehow get the four lovers to the wood.

Keep word, Lysander; we must starve our sight
From lovers' food till morrow deep midnight.
Lysander   I will, my Hermia.

Exit HERMIA

Helena adieu;
As you on him, Demetrius dote on you!   225

Exit LYSANDER

Helena
How happy some o'er other some can be!
Through Athens I am thought as fair as she.
But what of that? Demetrius thinks not so;
He will not know what all but he do know.
And as he errs, doting on Hermia's eyes,   230
So I, admiring of his qualities.
Things base and vile, holding no quantity,
Love can transpose to form and dignity.
Love looks not with the eyes, but with the mind;
And therefore is wing'd Cupid painted blind.   235
Nor hath Love's mind of any judgment taste;
Wings and no eyes figure unheedy haste;
And therefore is Love said to be a child,
Because in choice he is so oft beguil'd.
As waggish boys in game themselves forswear,   240
So the boy Love is perjur'd everywhere;
For ere Demetrius look'd on Hermia's eyne,
He hail'd down oaths that he was only mine;
And when this hail some heat from Hermia felt,
So he dissolv'd, and show'rs of oaths did melt.   245
I will go tell him of fair Hermia's flight;
Then to the wood will he to-morrow night
Pursue her; and for this intelligence
If I have thanks, it is a dear expense.
But herein mean I to enrich my pain,   250
To have his sight thither and back again.

Exit

SCENE II

This scene introduces *MND*'s clowns, the Athenian workmen/play-actors, a comic bunch – fat, skinny, tiny and tall – dressed in clothes that suggest their jobs. They are immensely vulgar, ignorant, and pleased with themselves; the joke is in the gap between their splendid plans and awful performances. There's no need to mind laughing at them because (like children or lovers) they live in their own world and see themselves as handsome, gifted, successful and clever. They talk, more or less all at once, in prose. Bottom, the bounciest and silliest of the lot, keeps taking over from the harassed Quince (an earnest man in spectacles) who has to try and keep him in some kind of order.

2. Bottom, who loves long words, often gets them wrong. Here, meaning 'severally' (one by one) he says *generally* (altogether).
3. *scrip:* paper (on which Quince has written the cast-list).
4. *scroll:* list.

5-6. *interlude:* short play.
6-7. *on his wedding-night at day:* 'on the evening of his wedding day'. The workmen's clumsy language is meant to amuse Shakespeare's upper-class audience.

8. *treats on:* 'is about'.

9-10. *grow to a point:* 'come to the point'.

11. *Marry:* indeed (short for 'by the Virgin Mary').
11-12. *most Lamentable Comedy and most Cruel Death:* Shakespeare is making fun of real Elizabethan plays whose titles mixed up comedy and tragedy. But perhaps the confusion is also meant to suggest that comedy and tragedy, like love and death (Act I, Scene i, lines 141-9) are close together – two sides of the same coin.
12. *Pyramus and Thisby:* a famous pair of ill-fated lovers. The play is put on in Act V.
15. *Masters:* gentlemen. A polite way to address the assembled company. Though Quince is the author and producer, it is Bottom who tells them all what to do. *spread yourselves:* they are all crowding round to see the cast list.

19. *tyrant:* a cruel violent king, or other splendid villain.

SCENE II—*Athens. Quince's house*

Enter QUINCE, SNUG, BOTTOM, FLUTE, SNOUT
and STARVELING

Quince
Is all our company here?

Bottom
You were best to call them generally, man by man,
according to the scrip.

Quince
Here is the scroll of every man's name which is
thought fit, through all Athens, to play in our inter-   5
lude before the Duke and the Duchess on his wedding-
day at night.

Bottom
First, good Peter Quince, say what the play treats on;
then read the names of the actors; and so grow to a
point.   10

Quince
Marry, our play is 'The most Lamentable Comedy
and most Cruel Death of Pyramus and Thisby.'

Bottom
A very good piece of work, I assure you, and a merry.
Now, good Peter Quince, call forth your actors by the
scroll. Masters, spread yourselves.   15

Quince
Answer, as I call you. Nick Bottom, the weaver.

Bottom
Ready. Name what part I am for, and proceed.

Quince
You, Nick Bottom, are set down for Pyramus.

Bottom
What is Pyramus? A lover, or a tyrant?

21-3. Bottom is sure he can move his audience. All the players expect their play to work like real life, causing sorrow, horror and fear.

23. *condole:* lament.

24. *humour:* fancy, inclination. 'I really fancy playing a tyrant best.' Bottom is carried away by the desire to scare his audience into fits, and Quince can't get a word in edgeways.

25. *Ercles:* Hercules, the Greek hero – a traditionally noisy and boisterous part. *tear a cat:* rant, rage and storm.

25-6. *make all split:* make a terrific row and split the listeners' ears.

27-34. '*The raging rocks . . . foolish Fates.*' Shakespeare immensely enjoyed sending up amateur plays and acting in general, and this example of Bottom's idea of good dramatic poetry is the first of many (see Act III, Scene i, lines 1-95 and Act V, Scene i, lines 126-346). No audience could be moved except to laughter by such stuff, but luckily the players don't realise this and remain perfectly happy and pleased with themselves throughout.

31. *Phibbus' car:* the chariot of Phoebus Apollo, the sun-god.

41. *wand'ring knight:* a 'knight errant' who in old stories wandered from place to place on adventures.

43-4. Elizabethan boys played women's parts, and Flute, with a beard and probably a deep voice to match it, is not well cast.

45-6. Ladies sometimes wore masks to protect their complexions – this will hide Flute's beard and if he speaks shrilly (*small*) all will be well.

Quince

    A lover, that kills himself most gallant for love.   *20*

Bottom

    That will ask some tears in the true performing of it.
    If I do it, let the audience look to their eyes; I will
    move storms; I will condole in some measure. To the
    rest—yet my chief humour is for a tyrant. I could
    play Ercles rarely, or a part to tear a cat in, to make   *25*
    all split.

>   'The raging rocks
>   And shivering shocks
>   Shall break the locks
>   Of prison gates;   *30*
>   And Phibbus' car
>   Shall shine from far,
>   And make and mar
>   The foolish Fates.'

    This was lofty. Now name the rest of the players.   *35*
    This is Ercles' vein, a tyrant's vein: a lover is more
    condoling.

Quince

    Francis Flute, the bellows-mender.

Flute

    Here, Peter Quince.

Quince

    Flute, you must take Thisby on you.   *40*

Flute

    What is Thisby? A wand'ring knight?

Quince

    It is the lady that Pyramus must love.

Flute

    Nay, faith, let not me play a woman; I have a beard
    coming.

Quince

    That's all one; you shall play it in a mask, and you   *45*
    may speak as small as you will.

48. *monstrous little:* 'mighty small'.

48-50. Bottom first imitates Pyramus calling Thisby in refined tones *'Thisne, Thisne!'*, and then puts on a shrill voice for Thisby's answer.

60. *the lion's part:* Shakespeare gets a lot of fun out of this pantomime lion, and it fascinates the players. Perhaps he's a comic counterpart to the wild animal passions that upset the lovers in the wood – they are saved from these, and the lion does not roar *too terribly* (line 70).

63. *slow of study:* a slow learner.

64. *extempore:* without preparation, 'off the cuff'.

67. *that:* so that.

Bottom

An I may hide my face, let me play Thisby too. I'll
speak in a monstrous little voice: 'Thisne, Thisne!'
[*Then speaking small*] 'Ah Pyramus, my lover dear!
Thy Thisby dear, and lady dear!'   50

Quince

No, no, you must play Pyramus; and, Flute, you
Thisby.

Bottom

Well, proceed.

Quince

Robin Starveling, the tailor.

Starveling

Here, Peter Quince.   55

Quince

Robin Starveling, you must play Thisby's mother.
Tom Snout, the tinker.

Snout

Here, Peter Quince.

Quince

You, Pyramus' father; myself, Thisby's father; Snug,
the joiner, you, the lion's part. And, I hope, here is a   60
play fitted.

Snug

Have you the lion's part written? Pray you, if it be,
give it me, for I am slow of study.

Quince

You may do it extempore, for it is nothing but
roaring.   65

Bottom

Let me play the lion too. I will roar that I will do any
man's heart good to hear me; I will roar that I will
make the Duke say 'Let him roar again, let him roar
again.'

Quince

An you should do it too terribly, you would fright the   70
Duchess and the ladies, that they would shriek; and

73. *every mother's son:* every one of us.

75. *discretion:* choice.
76. *aggravate:* strengthen, make louder. Bottom wants to say 'soften'.
77. *sucking dove:* baby dove.

79. *no part but Pyramus:* Bottom, losing himself in every part and imagining himself in a galaxy of beards (lines 86-9) may be a dreadfully bad actor, but he is a kind of poet too, *of imagination all compact* (Act V, Scene i, line 8).
80. *a proper man:* a fine handsome man.
81. *a summer's day:* a long day and so 'a long time'.

86. *discharge it:* act it. *your:* a (a colloquial way of speaking still sometimes used today, particularly by comic broadcasters).
86-9. Bottom as a weaver knows all about the colours cloths can be died, and can easily get hold of the materials for a false beard.
87. *orange-tawny:* tan. *purple-in-grain:* fast-dyed purple (probably dark red).

90-91. *A French crown* can be either a French gold coin, or a Frenchman's head. Quince is sick of Bottom's enthusiasm and makes a dry punning joke: baldness can be caused by venereal disease, supposed to be commonest among the amorous French.
93. *con them:* learn them by heart.

94. *the palace wood:* turns out to be the fairy-haunted wood where the lovers are to meet.

96. *we shall be dogg'd with company:* 'people won't let us alone'. Athens is crowded and public – lovers and artists have to escape.
97. *devices:* plans. *bill:* list.

that were enough to hang us all.

All

That would hang us, every mother's son.

Bottom

I grant you, friends, if you should fright the ladies out
of their wits, they would have no more discretion but 75
to hang us; but I will aggravate my voice so, that I
will roar you as gently as any sucking dove; I will
roar you an 'twere any nightingale.

Quince

You can play no part but Pyramus; for Pyramus is a
sweet-fac'd man; a proper man, as one shall see in a 80
summer's day; a most lovely gentleman-like man;
therefore you must needs play Pyramus.

Bottom

Well, I will undertake it. What beard were I best to
play it in?

Quince

Why, what you will. 85

Bottom

I will discharge it in either your straw-colour beard,
your orange-tawny beard, your purple-in-grain beard,
or your French-crown-colour beard, your perfect
yellow.

Quince

Some of your French crowns have no hair at all, and 90
then you will play bare-fac'd. But, masters, here are
your parts; and I am to entreat you, request you, and
desire you, to con them by to-morrow night; and
meet me in the palace wood, a mile without the town,
by moonlight; there will we rehearse; for if we meet 95
in the city, we shall be dogg'd with company, and
our devices known. In the meantime I will draw a bill
of properties, such as our play wants. I pray you, fail
me not.

101. *obscenely:* indecently. Heaven knows what Bottom thinks he's saying – 'privately' perhaps?

104. *hold, or cut bow-strings.* Disgraced archers had their bowstrings cut, so Bottom could mean 'keep your appointment' (*hold*) 'or be turned out of the play in disgrace'. Or perhaps *or cut bow-strings* means 'or give up the play', since an unrehearsed play would be no better than an unstrung bow.

Bottom

    We will meet; and there we may rehearse most *100*
obscenely and courageously. Take pains; be perfect;
adieu.

Quince

    At the Duke's oak we meet.

Bottom

    Enough; hold, or cut bow-strings.

                            Exeunt

ACT TWO

SCENE I

The atmosphere of the fairy wood – beautiful but wild and slightly sinister – is utterly different from Athens. It's moonlight, and a good modern production would get the effect with lighting; Shakespeare, in his own time, had to produce the effect with words alone. Puck and the Fairy set the scene – an open, out-of-doors world full of fairy mischief (where humans are likely to be at a disadvantage).

Act II should be unbroken: Scene ii carries straight on from Scene i. Oberon and Titania's quarrel comes to a head, and Oberon plans to revenge himself on Titania with the love-juice, which he administers in Scene ii. The four lovers all arrive, Demetrius and Helena quarrelling (Act II, Scene i, line 188), Lysander and Hermia lost but affectionate (Act II, Scene ii, line 35). Oberon plans to help with the love-juice but Puck puts it into the wrong lover's eyes and by the end of the act the lovers' affairs are in fine confusion.

1. 'Hey fairy, where are you going?' The fairies are spirits – supernatural, immortal, and (when they choose) invisible.
wander: the fairies are wild, free and restless, living out of doors. They are not tied down like human beings in houses and towns but come and go like the moon (lines 6-7).

2. *dale:* valley.

3. *Thorough:* through.

4. *pale:* private land shut in by a fence (the word is also applied to the fence itself).

7. The Elizabethans still thought that the earth stood still at the centre of the universe while the moon, sun, and other planets were whirled round it in hollow transparent globes called *spheres*. The sphere of the moon was nearest earth and so turned the quickest.

9. *dew her orbs:* 'water her fairy-rings'. Circles of greener grass (really caused by a fungus) are supposed to mark the fairies' dancing floors.
the green: the grassy fields.

10. *pensioners:* the royal bodyguard. To a fairy the cowslips are as tall as a man.

12. *fairy favours:* fairy gifts, the marks of love and goodwill.

13. *savours:* sweet smells.

15. Elizabethan gentlemen wore ear-rings.

16. *lob:* clumsy clown. Puck, unlike the other fairies, is both mischievous and rough.

17. *anon:* almost at once.

18. *revels:* wild gaieties with music, dancing and laughter.

20. *passing fell and wrath:* very fierce and angry.

23. *changeling:* a human child stolen as a baby by the fairies.

58

ACT TWO

SCENE I—*A wood near Athens*

Enter a FAIRY *at one door, and* PUCK *at another*

Puck
　　How now, spirit! whither wander you?
Fairy

　　　　Over hill, over dale,
　　　　　Thorough bush, thorough brier,
　　　　Over park, over pale,
　　　　　Thorough flood, thorough fire,　　　　　　　　*5*
　　　　I do wander every where,
　　　　Swifter than the moon's sphere;
　　　　And I serve the Fairy Queen,
　　　　To dew her orbs upon the green.
　　　　The cowslips tall her pensioners be;　　　　　*10*
　　　　In their gold coats spots you see;
　　　　Those be rubies, fairy favours,
　　　　In those freckles live their savours.

　　I must go seek some dewdrops here,
　　And hang a pearl in every cowslip's ear.　　　　　*15*
　　Farewell, thou lob of spirits; I'll be gone.
　　Our Queen and all her elves come here anon.
Puck
　　The King doth keep his revels here to-night;
　　Take heed the Queen come not within his sight;
　　For Oberon is passing fell and wrath,　　　　　　*20*
　　Because that she as her attendant hath
　　A lovely boy, stolen from an Indian king.
　　She never had so sweet a changeling;

24. Why should Oberon be *jealous* of Titania's love for the human child?

25. *train:* a king's or great nobleman's attendants. Oberon wants to bring the boy up as one of his courtiers. *trace:* range through.

26. *perforce:* forcibly.

28. *grove or green:* woodland or grassy place.

29. *spangled:* glittering. *sheen:* brilliant.

30. *square:* quarrel fiercely. (The expression 'square up' is used today of two men about to fight.)

31. *Creep into acorn cups.* The fairies are minute (far smaller than could be suggested by using children as actors). These tiny fairies quarrelling so fiercely in their own little world show how ridiculous human quarrels are.

32-57. Puck is a strange fairy, a mixture of household spirit, animal, demon, jester and actor. He is very wild and only Oberon can control him. He should be rough and shaggy-looking, though graceful, and he may wear little horns.

32. *making:* appearance.

33. *shrewd and knavish:* mischievous and naughty.

35. *maidens of the villagery:* village girls.

36. *quern:* hand-mill for grinding corn.

37. *bootless:* without result, uselessly.

38. *barm:* froth. Puck steals cream off the top of the milk, interferes with the grinding of the corn, and stops the butter coming and the ale fermenting.

39. He also acts as a will o' the wisp (a dancing light that can't be caught up with) to lead lost travellers astray by night. This is a cruel joke – human beings aren't quite real to Puck, who treats them like characters in a play put on to cause amusement. Notice too that all his delight is in confusion and disorder.

40. Robin Goodfellow is fond of nicknames like Hobgoblin (imp) and Puck (devil). (Originally a puck was a dangerous and frightening spirit, but Shakespeare makes him comic and fairly friendly.)

41. There are many tales about household fairies who work in return for kindness.

44. Puck is Oberon's court-jester. Since all his tricks and practical jokes depend on changes of shape and magical disguises, he could be called a kind of actor too.

45. *bean-fed:* vigorous. Puck cheats an eager stallion into thinking a young mare (*filly foal*) is calling him.

47. *lurk:* lie in ambush. *gossip:* sociable old woman.

48. *roasted crab:* hot crab-apple used to spice the ale.

50. *withered dewlap:* heavily wrinkled throat.

51. *aunt:* old woman. *saddest:* most serious.

52. *three-foot stool:* three-legged stool.

54. *'tailor':* a cry of surprise (it may have been customary to shout it at anyone who sat down suddenly on his 'tail').

55. *quire:* company.

56. *waxen in their mirth:* 'grow jollier and jollier'. *neeze:* sneeze.

57. *wasted:* spent.

58. *room:* clear out of the way.

And jealous Oberon would have the child
Knight of his train, to trace the forests wild;   25
But she perforce withholds the loved boy,
Crowns him with flowers, and makes him all her joy.
And now they never meet in grove or green,
By fountain clear, or spangled starlight sheen,
But they do square, that all their elves for fear   30
Creep into acorn cups and hide them there.

Fairy

Either I mistake your shape and making quite,
Or else you are that shrewd and knavish sprite
Call'd Robin Goodfellow. Are not you he
That frights the maidens of the villagery,   35
Skim milk, and sometimes labour in the quern,
And bootless make the breathless housewife churn,
And sometime make the drink to bear no barm,
Mislead night-wanderers, laughing at their harm?
Those that Hobgoblin call you, and sweet Puck,   40
You do their work, and they shall have good luck.
Are not you he?

Puck   Thou speakest aright:
I am that merry wanderer of the night.
I jest to Oberon, and make him smile
When I a fat and bean-fed horse beguile,   45
Neighing in likeness of a filly foal;
And sometime lurk I in a gossip's bowl
In very likeness of a roasted crab,
And, when she drinks, against her lips I bob,
And on her withered dewlap pour the ale.   50
The wisest aunt, telling the saddest tale,
Sometime for three-foot stool mistaketh me;
Then slip I from her bum, down topples she,
And 'tailor' cries, and falls into a cough;
And then the whole quire hold their hips and laugh,   55
And waxen in their mirth, and neeze, and swear
A merrier hour was never wasted there.
But room, fairy, here comes Oberon.

Stage Direction: Oberon and Titania, the king and queen in the wood, sweep on and meet as Theseus and Hippolyta did in Act I. But they frown instead of kissing and as Titania turns to go Oberon holds her back. Their quarrel has already been raging for some time and both are furious. They are the only married lovers in the play and their quarrelling is uglier than the young lovers'. As they rake up old scores against each other, spite, anger and jealousy stain everything they touch with evil. Pastoral beauty turns to a disguise for Oberon's adultery, and Theseus and Hippolyta themselves come under suspicion.

60-1. *Proud* and *jealous* both have the second meaning 'lustful', 'sensual'. Proud also means 'swollen' – Titania has got too big for her boots and thrown off Oberon's authority.

62. *forsworn:* completely given up. Titania utterly refuses either to sleep with her husband or to spend time with him.

63. *Tarry, rash wanton:* 'Wait, reckless rebel'. *Rash* can also mean 'hot' and *wanton* a loose woman.

63-73. Oberon is angry because Titania does not obey him as a wife should: she hints in reply that he can't expect obedience when he is unfaithful to her. They are quarrelling now over two of the commonest problems in marriage – authority and sexual loyalty.

66. The fairies, who are usually invisible to mortals, can take on human appearance if they like (as the old gods did when they fell in love with mortal women).

66-8. *Corin* and *Phillida* are lovers in Elizabethan pastoral (poetry about shepherds and shepherdesses living the perfect country life).

67. *versing love:* telling his love in a song or poem.

69. *steep:* mountain slope. *India:* the fairies have an exotic Eastern side to them, as well as a homely English one.

70. *bouncing:* big and clumsy. Titania scornfully compares the powerful soldier queen with herself.

71. *buskin'd:* booted. A buskin is a calf or knee-length boot worn for battle or hunting.

73. 'To bless them with happy marriage and fine children.'

74-6. Oberon turns the tables on Titania by accusing her of loving Theseus.

75. *Glance at my credit:* 'cast suspicion on my reputation'.

77. *glimmering:* faintly shining (the half-light of a starry night without a moon goes well with shady goings-on).

78-80. *Perigouna, Aegles, Ariadne, Antiopa:* lovers of Theseus. Though Shakespeare presents Theseus as a wise and virtuous prince on the point of marriage, he was notorious in classical stories for his love-affairs and betrayals of women. No-one's sexual behaviour in *MND* is perfectly well-regulated, if even Theseus was promiscuous before marriage.

81. *forgeries:* inventions. Whether true or false, these accusations cast a shadow over Hippolyta and Theseus as well as Oberon and Titania themselves. Happiness in *MND* is won through disturbance and confusion and no-one has a blameless past.

81-117. Now as Titania describes the bad effects of their quarrel we see the fairy king and queen in a new light. They are powerful mysterious nature spirits, more like primitive gods than what we mean by fairies,

Fairy
And here my mistress. Would that he were gone!

Enter OBERON *at one door, with his* TRAIN,
and TITANIA, *at another, with hers*

Oberon
Ill met by moonlight, proud Titania.   60
Titania
What, jealous Oberon! Fairies, skip hence;
I have forsworn his bed and company.
Oberon
Tarry, rash wanton; am not I thy lord?
Titania This is said
Then I must be thy lady; but I know
When thou hast stolen away from fairy land,   65
And in the shape of Corin sat all day,
Playing on pipes of corn, and versing love
To amorous Phillida. Why art thou here,
Come from the farthest steep of India,
But that, forsooth, the bouncing Amazon,   70
Your buskin'd mistress and your warrior love,
To Theseus must be wedded, and you come
To give their bed joy and prosperity?
Oberon
How canst thou thus, for shame, Titania,
Glance at my credit with Hippolyta,   75
Knowing I know thy love to Theseus?
Didst not thou lead him through the glimmering night
From Perigouna, whom he ravished?
And make him with fair Ægles break his faith,
With Ariadne and Antiopa?   80
Titania
These are the forgeries of jealousy;

and on their sexual harmony and love the weather, the seasons, the harvest and all natural processes depend.

82. *middle summer's spring:* the beginning of midsummer.

83. *mead:* meadow.

84. *paved fountain:* a stony spring, in contrast to a muddy brook where rushes grow. Titania quarrels with Oberon wherever in the countryside she meets him.

85. *in:* on. *beached margent:* the sea's edge where there's a beach suitable for dancing.

87. *brawls:* rows.

88. *piping to us:* 'playing for us to dance'. The winds are angry and waste their energy in destruction when the fairies quarrel instead of dancing to their music. For the Elizabethans dancing stood for harmony, love and marriage, and the fairy dance is the source of harmony and fertility in nature.

90. *Contagious:* unhealthy.

91. *pelting:* little and unimportant. *proud:* swollen full of water (as well as 'pleased with themselves').

92. Instead of keeping in their proper places the rivers have overflowed their banks – everything in nature is breaking out of bounds.

93-4. The ploughman and his ox have both worked hard for nothing, for the wet has ruined the corn.

94-5. The young (*green*) corn has rotted before it was ripe. The crops have not come to harvest, and instead of healthy growth and ripeness there is barren waste. *a beard:* ripe ears of corn are bristly and hairy-looking.

96. *fold:* sheep-fold. *drowned:* flooded.

97. Crows feast on heaps of animals dead of cattle-disease (*murrion* or murrain) caused by the wet.

98. *nine men's morris:* a game something like draughts or checkers on a large scale, played on a 'board' cut out in the grass, and now reduced to mud by the rain. (The nearest modern equivalent is perhaps childrens' hop-scotch.)

99-100. The intricate little paths (*quaint mazes:* either sheep-paths or the track of a running-game) in the long lush grass (*wanton green*), usually kept open by being walked on, have vanished.

101. *want:* lack. Though it's summer the weather is wintry, and some editors suggest *here* should be read 'cheer' ('Christmas celebrations are needed to cheer things up') or 'gear' ('winter clothes'). But no one really knows what this line means.

102. *carol:* need not be a Christmas carol, it could be a May-time or summer song.

103. *Therefore* refers right back to line 88. The moon, like the winds, is angry because the fairy dance is spoilt. *governess of floods:* ruler of tides and flooding.

104. The moon is hostile to life and shines pale through the foggy air. *washes:* with heavy dew and rain, like tears.

105. *rheumatic diseases:* colds and coughs.

106. *distemperature:* disturbed unhealthy weather.

107. *hoary-headed:* white-haired.

And never, since the middle summer's spring,
Met we on hill, in dale, forest, or mead,
By paved fountain, or by rushy brook,
Or in the beached margent of the sea,   *85*
To dance our ringlets to the whistling wind,
But with thy brawls thou hast disturb'd our sport.
Therefore the winds, piping to us in vain,
As in revenge, have suck'd up from the sea
Contagious fogs; which, falling in the land,   *90*
Hath every pelting river made so proud
That they have overborne their continents.
The ox hath therefore stretch'd his yoke in vain,
The ploughman lost his sweat, and the green corn
Hath rotted ere his youth attain'd a beard;   *95*
The fold stands empty in the drowned field,
And crows are fatted with the murrion flock;
The nine men's morris is fill'd up with mud,
And the quaint mazes in the wanton green,
For lack of tread, are undistinguishable.   *100*
The human mortals want their winter here;
No night is now with hymn or carol blest;
Therefore the moon, the governess of floods,
Pale in her anger, washes all the air,
That rheumatic diseases do abound.   *105*
And thorough this distemperature we see
The seasons alter: hoary-headed frosts

109. *Hiems:* winter. *crown:* head (*thin* because Winter is an old man and nearly bald).
110. *odorous chaplet:* sweet-smelling wreath. An unnaturally mild winter seems to have followed an extremely wet, cold summer.
112. *childing:* fertile, fruitful.

113. *wonted liveries:* usual clothes.
113-14. Crops (*increase*) no longer grow at the proper time, so everyone is too bewildered (*mazed*) to tell the seasons apart.
115. *progeny:* swarm, brood. Oberon and Titania's quarrel has given birth to swarms of troubles.
116. *debate:* quarrel. *dissension:* disagreement.
117. *original:* origin. Titania feels guilty.

118. *amend it:* set it right.

121. *henchman:* page.

123. *a vot'ress of my order:* 'one of my devout worshippers'. (Again, Titania is treated as a goddess.)
124. *spiced:* spicy-smelling.

126. *Neptune's yellow sands:* the seashore. Neptune was the sea god.
127. 'Watching the merchant ships sailing by on the water.'
128-34. Titania and her friend were amused when the wind caused the ships' sails to swell out like pregnant women, and then the big-bellied woman herself carried on the joke by pretending to be a ship.
129. *wanton:* amorous.
130. *swimming gait:* gliding walk.
131. She was carrying Titania's little pageboy in her womb at the time.

135. Titania tenderly remembers their shared delight in fertility and motherhood, but her voice changes sharply as she comes to the woman's death in childbed. Though she is immortal the fairy queen is herself childless, and she is both fascinated by human fertility and troubled by human death.

138. Oberon ignores Titania's emotion (as in a human quarrel, the woman has done most of the talking). Whose side would you take now you have heard her explanation – and whose side do you suppose an Elizabethan audience would take?

Fall in the fresh lap of the crimson rose;
And on old Hiems' thin and icy crown
An odorous chaplet of sweet summer buds   *110*
Is, as in mockery, set. The spring, the summer,
The childing autumn, angry winter, change
Their wonted liveries; and the mazed world,
By their increase, now knows not which is which.
And this same progeny of evils comes   *115*
From our debate, from our dissension;
We are their parents and original.

Oberon
Do you amend it, then; it lies in you.
Why should Titania cross her Oberon?
I do but beg a little changeling boy   *120*
To be my henchman.

Titania   Set your heart at rest;
The fairy land buys not the child of me.
His mother was a vot'ress of my order;
And, in the spiced Indian air, by night,
Full often hath she gossip'd by my side;   *125*
And sat with me on Neptune's yellow sands,
Marking th' embarked traders on the flood;
When we have laugh'd to see the sails conceive,
And grow big-bellied with the wanton wind;
Which she, with pretty and with swimming gait   *130*
Following—her womb then rich with my young
    squire—
Would imitate, and sail upon the land,
To fetch me trifles, and return again,
As from a voyage, rich with merchandise.
But she, being mortal, of that boy did die;   *135*
And for her sake do I rear up her boy;
And for her sake I will not part with him.

Oberon
How long within this wood intend you stay?

Titania
Perchance till after Theseus' wedding-day.

140. *patiently:* without causing a disturbance. *dance in our round:* 'join in our round-dances'.

142. *shun:* avoid. *spare your haunts:* keep clear of your favourite spots.

145. *chide downright:* 'have a real row'.

146. *thou shalt . . . grove:* 'You shan't leave this wood.'

147. *torment:* torture, tease severely. Oberon is cool but spiteful.

149. *Since:* when. *promontory:* headland sticking out into the sea.

150-4. Oberon's description of this lovely music seems out of place when he's just about to punish Titania unkindly. But his action brings back harmony and love – which music creates – and it is right to remind us of these just before the confusions of the love-juice plot. Notice how the whole story of the juice's origin is deliberately told (lines 148-68) in a distant and beautiful way.
151. 'Singing so sweetly and melodiously.'
152-3. The music had such soothing and attractive powers that it calmed the sea and drew the stars out of the sky. *rude:* rough. *civil:* well-behaved. (*spheres:* see line 7.)

156. *cold:* chaste. Here the moon is again love's enemy.

157. *all arm'd:* with his bow and golden arrows.

158. *vestal:* a woman who has vowed to remain a virgin. These lines (158-64) which show virginity as dignified and noble, may be meant as a compliment to Queen Elizabeth I, who never married. They contrast with the rest of the play's championship of marriage as the best and most natural way of life.
159-62. Cupid shot off his arrow vigorously but the moon's cold rays put out its fire.
163. *imperial vot'ress:* royal servant of chastity.

164. 'Deep in her own solitary thoughts, uninfluenced by love.'

165. 'I noticed where Cupid's arrow fell.'

167. *purple:* the colour of blood (drawn by the arrow) and of passion.

168. *Love-in-idleness:* the wild pansy or heartsease.

If you will patiently dance in our round,   140
And see our moonlight revels, go with us;
If not, shun me, and I will spare your haunts.

Oberon

Give me that boy and I will go with thee.

Titania

Not for thy fairy kingdom. Fairies, away.
We shall chide downright if I longer stay.   145

Exit TITANIA *with her* TRAIN

Oberon

Well, go thy way; thou shalt not from this grove
Till I torment thee for this injury.
My gentle Puck, come hither. Thou rememb'rest
Since once I sat upon a promontory,
And heard a mermaid on a dolphin's back   150
Uttering such dulcet and harmonious breath
That the rude sea grew civil at her song,
And certain stars shot madly from their spheres
To hear the sea-maid's music.

Puck   I remember.

Oberon

That very time I saw, but thou couldst not,   155
Flying between the cold moon and the earth
Cupid, all arm'd; a certain aim he took
At a fair vestal, throned by the west,
And loos'd his love-shaft smartly from his bow,
As it should pierce a hundred thousand hearts; 160
But I might see young Cupid's fiery shaft
Quench'd in the chaste beams of the wat'ry moon;
And the imperial vot'ress passed on,
In maiden meditation, fancy-free.
Yet mark'd I where the bolt of Cupid fell.   165
It fell upon a little western flower,
Before milk-white, now purple with love's wound,
And maidens call it Love-in-idleness.
Fetch me that flow'r, the herb I showed thee once.

170. *The juice of it.* The blood of the flower wounded by love is a kind of concentrated love essence or aphrodisiac.

171. *or . . . or:* either . . . or.

171-2. *madly dote upon:* wildly in love with.

174. 'At top speed.' *leviathan:* a huge biblical sea-monster, thought by the Elizabethans to be a whale.

175. 'I'll fly right round the world.' *girdle:* belt. Fairies aren't tied by the ordinary laws of nature, and Puck can fly faster than the fastest jet.

176-85. In Elizabethan marriage, the husband stood for the soul and reason (the distinctively human part of man), the wife for the body and passion. When she threw off her husband's authority Titania refused the rule of reason, and so Oberon means to punish her by giving her up to her own unreasonable physical desires. She refuses to love her husband – very well, left alone she'll fall helplessly in love with an animal.

177. *when she is asleep:* and so 'when her conscious mind isn't in control'.

178. Since it's how you see that decides what you approve of, Oberon doctors Titania's eyes.

179. 'Then, whatever she sees first when she wakes . . .' Love strikes at first sight through the eyes.

182. *the soul of love:* the fiercest desire.

185. Titania will be too wrapped up in her lover to care about the child (this happens, Act IV, Scene i, lines 57-61).

186. *I am invisible.* Since the audience can see Oberon, he has to remind them that the lovers can't. He withdraws to one side of the stage, perhaps wrapping his cloak around him, and standing quite still.

187. *conference:* conversation. The lovers in the wood are funny rather than dignified – specially since they take themselves intensely seriously. Helena has carried out her plan and told Demetrius of Hermia's flight with Lysander. Demetrius is desperate, what with rage at Lysander, worry in case he loses Hermia, and irritation at the clinging Helena. He speaks roughly and impatiently. Helena is plaintively determined to hang on to him, and even gets a perverse pleasure out of his roughness. Her voice sounds slightly sentimental and self-pitying. Of course, they can't see Oberon.

190. *slayeth me:* Hermia's scorn is 'killing' Demetrius. Notice love and death close together again – love when it's unrequited hurts like death.

192. *wood:* mad. There is more truth in this than Demetrius knows. Love is a kind of madness (lines 153 and 171), and everything happens madly in the wood till the mortals escape back to Athens and daylight.

194-202. The behaviour of Hermia and Demetrius bears out Act I, Scene i, line 199, *The more I love, the more he hateth me.* She is besotted and completely unreasonable – the plainest truth that he doesn't and can't love her only makes her love him more.

195. *adamant:* a very hard stone (like Demetrius' heart) and a magnet (as he is to Helena).

196-7. These lines seem to have a complicated double meaning:
(i) 'the heart you attract isn't any second-rate metal, it's true as the finest steel.'

The juice of it on sleeping eyelids laid   *170*
Will make or man or woman madly dote
Upon the next live creature that it sees.
Fetch me this herb, and be thou here again
Ere the leviathan can swim a league.

Puck
I'll put a girdle round about the earth   *175*
In forty minutes.

Exit PUCK

Oberon   Having once this juice,
I'll watch Titania when she is asleep,
And drop the liquor of it in her eyes;
The next thing then she waking looks upon,
Be it on lion, bear, or wolf, or bull,   *180*
On meddling monkey, or on busy ape,
She shall pursue it with the soul of love.
And ere I take this charm from off her sight,
As I can take it with another herb,
I'll make her render up her page to me.   *185*
But who comes here? I am invisible;
And I will overhear their conference.

Enter DEMETRIUS, HELENA *following him*

Demetrius
I love thee not, therefore pursue me not.
Where is Lysander and fair Hermia?
The one I'll slay, the other slayeth me.   *190*
Thou told'st me they were stol'n unto this wood,
And here am I, and wood within this wood,
Because I cannot meet my Hermia.
Hence, get thee gone, and follow me no more.

Helena
You draw me, you hard-hearted adamant;   *195*
But yet you draw not iron, for my heart

(ii) 'you have no excuse to kill me (*you draw not iron*=you don't draw your sword) because I'm perfectly faithful' (*true as steel* (197).

199. *entice:* 'lead you on'. *speak you fair:* 'speak to you kindly'.

201. 'I don't love you and I never shall.' Angry irritation makes Demetrius speak plainly and shortly. He barks at her.

203. *spaniel:* these sentimental dogs are supposed to love even a cruel master ('a spaniel, a woman and a walnut tree, the more you beat them, the better they be'). Love has made Helena like a silly animal.
204. *fawn:* behave very subserviently, 'crawl'.
205. *spurn me:* 'push me away'.

209. 'A valuable position in my eyes.' Helena 'crawls' to Demetrius to try and make him love her.

211-12. Lovers' feelings are violent and extreme, and where they don't love, they hate.

214. *impeach your modesty:* 'dirty your good name'.

218. *ill-counsel:* bad advice. *desert:* lonely.

220. 'You are too good to harm me.' Helena calls Demetrius's bluff, and refuses to take seriously his threat to rape her.
221-6. Love's inner power is stronger than outside fact. For Helena, the sight of Demetrius turns night to day, and as he's all the world to her, how can she be alone? (But by the end of the night the facts of anger, darkness and exhaustion are too much for all the lovers. (See, e.g., Act III, Scene ii, lines 432-6.)
224. *respect:* view.

Is true as steel. Leave you your power to draw,
And I shall have no power to follow you.

Demetrius

Do I entice you? Do I speak you fair?
Or, rather, do I not in plainest truth   200
Tell you I do not nor I cannot love you?

Helena

And even for that do I love you the more.
I am your spaniel; and, Demetrius,
The more you beat me, I will fawn on you.
Use me but as your spaniel, spurn me, strike me,   205
Neglect me, lose me; only give me leave,
Unworthy as I am, to follow you.
What worser place can I beg in your love,
And yet a place of high respect with me,
Than to be used as you use your dog?   210

Demetrius

Tempt not too much the hatred of my spirit;
For I am sick when I do look on thee.

Helena

And I am sick when I look not on you.

Demetrius

You do impeach your modesty too much
To leave the city and commit yourself   215
Into the hands of one that loves you not;
To trust the opportunity of night,
And the ill counsel of a desert place,
With the rich worth of your virginity.

Helena

Your virtue is my privilege for that: 220
It is not night when I do see your face,
Therefore I think I am not in the night;
Nor doth this wood lack worlds of company,
For you, in my respect, are all the world.
Then how can it be said I am alone   225
When all the world is here to look on me?

73

227. *brakes:* thick bushes.

229. Now it's Demetrius who's harder-hearted than a wild animal. People in love scarcely behave like human beings.

230-1. Helena jeers at Demetrius: once the sun god *Apollo* chased the nymph *Daphne*, now it's the other way about and the girl does the chasing (*holds the chase*) after the boy.

232-4. Things are changed indeed if the peaceful *dove* and gentle female deer (*mild hind*) chase the dangerous *griffin* (an imaginary winged beast with eagle's head, lion's body and serpent's tail) and the *tiger.*

235. *stay thy questions:* 'wait while you talk'.

236-7. 'You can be sure I'll harm you.' Demetrius means he'll attack her, but Helena replies that he already hurts her feelings and reputation everywhere.

240. *set a scandal on my sex:* 'damage the good reputation of women in general'.

242. It is not natural for a woman to have to run after a man, and it's particularly disconcerting for the passive and dependent Helena. Their situation comically reverses the usual one, but she doesn't see it as funny. Oberon, overhearing, plans to put things right and at the same time get some fun out of making Demetrius chase Helena more ardently than even she would enjoy (lines 245-6). (This happens later when, thinking he's only pretending to love her again, she rejects his advances: Act III, Scene ii, line 145.) *woo:* Helena's voice rises to an indignant howl as Demetrius dashes off. Do you entirely blame him for wanting to escape?

245. *nymph:* Oberon uses the word in a sarcastic way.

249. *thyme:* a sweet-smelling herb. *blows:* flowers, blooms.

250. *oxlips:* wild flowers like large cowslips.

Demetrius
  I'll run from thee and hide me in the brakes,
  And leave thee to the mercy of wild beasts.
Helena
  The wildest hath not such a heart as you.
  Run when you will; the story shall be chang'd: 230
  Apollo flies, and Daphne holds the chase;
  The dove pursues the griffin; the mild hind
  Makes speed to catch the tiger—bootless speed,
  When cowardice pursues and valour flies.
Demetrius
  I will not stay thy questions; let me go;   235
  Or, if thou follow me, do not believe
  But I shall do thee mischief in the wood.
Helena
  Ay, in the temple, in the town, the field,
  You do me mischief. Fie, Demetrius!
  Your wrongs do set a scandal on my sex.   240
  We cannot fight for love as men may do;
  We should be woo'd, and were not made to woo.

Exit DEMETRIUS

  I'll follow thee, and make a heaven of hell,
  To die upon the hand I love so well.

Exit HELENA

Oberon
  Fare thee well, nymph; ere he do leave this grove,   245
  Thou shalt fly him, and he shall seek thy love.

Re-enter PUCK

  Hast thou the flower there? Welcome wanderer.
Puck
  Ay, there it is.
Oberon   I pray thee give it me.
  I know a bank where the wild thyme blows,
  Where oxlips and the nodding violet grows,   250

75

251. *woodbine:* honeysuckle; it overhangs the bank like a tent.

252. *musk roses* and *eglantine:* two roses cultivated by the Elizabethans.

253. *sometime:* for some part of.

254. *Lull'd:* soothed asleep (in the next scene her fairies sing Titania to sleep).

256. *Weed wide enough . . . in:* 'a large enough dress for a fairy'. As a snake grows it forms a new skin beneath the old which is then cast off. Titania, wrapped in a snake-skin, her mind full of animal fantasies, herself almost becomes a snake among the flowers.
257. *streak* ('touch gently'): also implies that Titania's sight will be striped and distorted with evil.
258. *hateful fantasies:* disgusting false desires and imaginings. These venomous lines (257-8) are suddenly shocking after the delicate picture of Titania's flowery bed.

264. Oberon doesn't know that other people in Athenian dress are about, whose eyes may get treated with the magic liquid by mistake.
265. *Effect . . . care:* 'do it carefully'.

SCENE II

There is no need for a scene-break here. If a bower for Titania is wanted it can be a permanent structure at the back of the stage.

1. *roundel:* dance in a ring.

3. *cankers:* rose-eating caterpillars.

4. *rere-mice:* bats. *leathern:* made of leather.

6. *clamorous:* noisy. *nightly:* every night.
7. *quaint:* 'strange', but also 'fine' and 'neat'.
8. *offices:* duties. These little tasks, done in twenty seconds, a long time to a fairy, show them as tiny, dainty, supernaturally quick – and also cruel, fighting for their lives in the violent world of nature.

Quite over-canopied with luscious woodbine,
With sweet musk-roses, and with eglantine;
There sleeps Titania sometime of the night,
Lull'd in these flowers with dances and delight;
And there the snake throws her enamell'd skin,   *255*
Weed wide enough to wrap a fairy in;
And with the juice of this I'll streak her eyes,
And make her full of hateful fantasies.
Take thou some of it, and seek through this grove:
A sweet Athenian lady is in love   *260*
With a disdainful youth; anoint his eyes;
But do it when the next thing he espies
May be the lady. Thou shalt know the man
By the Athenian garments he hath on.
Effect it with some care, that he may prove   *265*
More fond on her than she upon her love.
And look thou meet me ere the first cock crow.

Puck

Fear not, my lord; your servant shall do so.

Exeunt

SCENE II—*Another part of the wood*

Enter TITANIA, *with her* TRAIN

Titania

Come now, a roundel and a fairy song;
Then, for the third part of a minute, hence:
Some to kill cankers in the musk-rose buds;
Some war with rere-mice for their leathern wings,
To make my small elves coats; and some keep back   *5*
The clamorous owl that nightly hoots and wonders
At our quaint spirits. Sing me now asleep;
Then to your offices, and let me rest.

9. *spotted snakes with double tongue:* snakes with forked tongues and mottled skins. (Snakes were thought of as specially dangerous and treacherous, not only because of their poison, but because it was the snake that tempted Eve in the *Genesis* story.)

11. *blind-worms:* small snake-like lizards, wrongly thought (as with newts and spiders) to be poisonous. Certainly all these creatures might be dangerous to a fairy.

13. *Philomel:* the nightingale.

18. *nigh:* near.

23. *offence:* harm.

26. *aloof:* at a distance. *stand sentinel:* keep guard. Though the spell of protection keeps dangerous animals away it can't keep out Oberon — or Titania's own thoughts once he has treated her eyes with the juice.

27-34. Oberon's spell is sinister and menacing after the half-playful fairy song.

29. *languish:* waste away with longing.

30. *ounce:* lynx. *cat:* wild cat.

31. *Pard:* panther or leopard. *bristled:* bristly, prickly (suggesting sexual vigour).

The FAIRIES *sing*

1st. Fairy

> You spotted snakes with double tongue,
> Thorny hedgehogs, be not seen;   10
> Newts and blind-worms, do no wrong,
> Come not near our fairy Queen.

Chorus

> Philomel with melody
> Sing in our sweet lullaby.
> Lulla, lulla, lullaby; lulla, lulla, lullaby.   15
> Never harm
> Nor spell nor charm
> Come our lovely lady nigh.
> So good night, with lullaby.

2nd. Fairy

> Weaving spiders, come not here;   20
> Hence, you long-legg'd spinners, hence.
> Beetles black, approach not near;
> Worm nor snail do no offence.

Chorus

> Philomel with melody, etc.

TITANIA sleeps

1st. Fairy

> Hence away; now all is well.   25
> One aloof stand sentinel.

Exeunt FAIRIES
Enter OBERON *and squeezes the flower on*
TITANIA'S *eyelids*

Oberon

What thou seest when thou dost wake,
Do it for thy true-love take;
Love and languish for his sake.
Be it ounce, or cat, or bear,   30
Pard, or boar with bristled hair,

33. *dear:* love, dear one.

Stage Direction: As Titania sleeps unnoticed in the background, Lysander and Hermia enter lost and tired. Though elopement has turned out exhausting rather than romantic they are tender and considerate towards each other. Their conversation is true dialogue (unlike Helena's and Lysander's cross-talk), they exchange ideas and alter their behaviour to fit in with each other. But their concern for each other in what is the play's nearest approach to a bedroom scene, can be funny as well as touching, as they come together, spring apart, and finally lie down to sleep at opposite sides of the stage. (In this episode, lines 35-156, the lovers begin to swap partners – by the end of the scene, Lysander has left Hermia to chase Helena.)

35. *you faint:* 'you're getting tired and depressed'.

36. *to speak troth:* to tell the truth.

41. *turf:* patch of short grass.

42. *troth:* promise to love each other.

45-6. Lysander is offended because Hermia suspects his intentions – since love teaches lovers to grasp each other's true meaning, she must know he means nothing but good. *love's conference:* lovers' talk.

49. *interchained with an oath:* 'tied together by a solemn promise'.

52. 'When I lie down beside you, Hermia, I shan't act in any wrong way.'

53. *riddles.* The lovers can talk playfully because they trust each other.

54. *much beshrew:* many curses on. Hermia isn't distrustful, she's just modest (though perhaps she knows Lysander better than he knows himself).

58-60. Though she's run away with Lysander Hermia still cares about society's moral rules – and even 'what people think'.

In thy eye that shall appear
When thou wak'st, it is thy dear.
Wake when some vile thing is near.

Exit
Enter LYSANDER *and* HERMIA

Lysander

Fair love, you faint with wand'ring in the wood;   35
And, to speak troth, I have forgot our way;
We'll rest us, Hermia, if you think it good,
And tarry for the comfort of the day.

Hermia

Be it so, Lysander: find you out a bed,
For I upon this bank will rest my head.   40

Lysander

One turf shall serve as pillow for us both;
One heart, one bed, two bosoms, and one troth.

Hermia

Nay, good Lysander; for my sake, my dear,
Lie further off yet; do not lie so near.

Lysander

O, take the sense, sweet, of my innocence!   45
Love takes the meaning in love's conference.
I mean that my heart unto yours is knit,
So that but one heart we can make of it;
Two bosoms interchained with an oath,
So then two bosoms and a single troth.   50
Then by your side no bed-room me deny,
For lying so, Hermia, I do not lie.

Hermia

Lysander riddles very prettily.
Now much beshrew my manners and my pride,
If Hermia meant to say Lysander lied!   55
But, gentle friend, for love and courtesy
Lie further off, in human modesty;
Such separation as may well be said

61-3. Lysander will wake to fall madly in love with Helena and leave Hermia in the lurch. Under the influence of the magic juice the lovers' violent declarations of undying love (or hate) keep getting comically reversed.

62. *Amen:* 'so be it'.

65. 'I return your last wish: may you sleep well, too.'

68. *approve:* try out.

69. *force in stirring:* power to stir up.

70. Puck can find nothing but *Night and silence*; then suddenly he comes across Lysander, in Athenian clothes, and thinks it's Demetrius.

75. *dank:* damp and nasty.

76. *durst:* dare.

77. *lack-love . . . kill-courtesy:* rude, unloving man. Puck, who knows nothing about *human modesty* (line 57) and would think it very silly if he did, thinks Lysander is unkind to sleep away from Hermia.

78. *Churl:* brute.

79. 'All this charm's power.' (*owe*=own.)

80-1. *let love . . . eyelid:* 'may love drive sleep away from you'. Puck's mistake would be harmless, but at this moment Demetrius and Helena rush in, and Demetrius promptly rushes out again, leaving Helena behind to wake Lysander . . .

85. 'Clear off and leave me alone!'

Becomes a virtuous bachelor and a maid,
So far be distant; and good night, sweet friend.   *60*
Thy love ne'er alter till thy sweet life end!

Lysander
Amen, amen, to that fair prayer say I;
And then end life when I end loyalty!
Here is my bed; sleep give thee all his rest!

Hermia
With half that wish the wisher's eyes be press'd!   *65*

They sleep
Enter PUCK

Puck
 Through the forest have I gone,
 But Athenian found I none
 On whose eyes I might approve
 This flower's force in stirring love.
 Night and silence—Who is here?   *70*
 Weeds of Athens he doth wear:
 This is he, my master said,
 Despised the Athenian maid;
 And here the maiden, sleeping sound,
 On the dank and dirty ground.   *75*
 Pretty soul! she durst not lie
 Near this lack-love, this kill-courtesy.
 Churl, upon thy eyes I throw
 All the power this charm doth owe:
 When thou wak'st let love forbid   *80*
 Sleep his seat on thy eyelid.
 So awake when I am gone;
 For I must now to Oberon.

Exit
Enter DEMETRIUS *and* HELENA, *running*

Helena
Stay, though thou kill me, sweet Demetrius.

Demetrius
I charge thee, hence, and do not haunt me thus.   *85*

86. *darkling:* in the dark. Helena is scared.

87. 'Stay here or you'll get hurt; I'm going by myself.'

88. *fond:* 'loving', but also 'silly'.

89. 'The more I ask the less I get.'

90. *Happy:* lucky. Helena is miserably jealous of Hermia.

95. It's not surprising that Helena scares the wild animals, considering the noise she makes. Demetrius' dislike has undermined her self-confidence and she's beginning to hate herself because he won't love her. She feels as ugly as a brute and can't believe her face is really beautiful, as it looked in the mirror (lines 98-9).

96-7. 'No wonder Demetrius runs away from me like this as though I were a monster.' It's love that has monstrous effects if it can make pretty Helena believe she is one.

98-9. Helena's mirror (*glass*) tricked her into thinking herself as good-looking as Hermia. *dissembling:* pretending.

99. *sphery eyne:* starry eyes.

100-3. Helena at last notices Lysander and wakes him to see if he's dead. Of course the magic juice works instantly and he springs up with a passionate declaration of love. The rhyme split between the two speakers (*awake . . . sake*) makes his response seem much quicker and funnier.

104. *Transparent:* clear as glass, diamond or crystal, and so 'beautiful', and also 'open, candid'. Lysander means that Helena's lovely body reveals her lovely soul.

104-5. *Nature shows art . . .* The picture this calls up of Helena with a glass-fronted chest is meant to be faintly ridiculous. Lysander's exaggerated praise of Helena is different from his more natural conversation with Hermia whom he knows and really loves (though all the lovers use an elaborate style except when they're enraged). Of course, Lysander is never further from seeing into Helena's heart, for he's just fallen into the kind of blind love that ignores what its object is really like. Throughout his wooing of Helena he takes no notice of what she says at all.

108-10. Helena hasn't caught up with Lysander's changed feelings yet; she thinks he's angry because Demetrius loves Hermia

110. *be content:* 'don't worry'.

111. *Content:* satisfied.

112. *tedious:* boring.

113-14. The *raven* is a black bird (dark Hermia), the *dove* (blonde Helena) a white one. Love sees things in black and white, and to Lysander if Helena's lovely then Hermia (whom a few hours ago he worshipped) must be ugly as a crow.

84

Helena
O, wilt thou darkling leave me? Do not so.
Demetrius
Stay on thy peril; I alone will go.

Exit DEMETRIUS

Helena
O, I am out of breath in this fond chase!
The more my prayer, the lesser is my grace.
Happy is Hermia, wheresoe'er she lies,   *90*
For she hath blessed and attractive eyes.
How came her eyes so bright? Not with salt tears;
If so, my eyes are oft'ner wash'd than hers.
No, no, I am as ugly as a bear,
For beasts that meet me run away for fear;   *95*
Therefore no marvel though Demetrius
Do, as a monster, fly my presence thus.
What wicked and dissembling glass of mine
Made me compare with Hermia's sphery eyne?
But who is here? Lysander! on the ground!   *100*
Dead, or asleep? I see no blood, no wound.
Lysander, if you live, good sir, awake.
Lysander [*Waking*]
And run through fire I will for thy sweet sake.
Transparent Helena! Nature shows art,
That through thy bosom makes me see thy heart.   *105*
Where is Demetrius? O, how fit a word
Is that vile name to perish on my sword!
Helena
Do not say so, Lysander; say not so.
What though he love your Hermia? Lord, what
    though?
Yet Hermia still loves you; then be content.   *110*
Lysander
Content with Hermia! No: I do repent
The tedious minutes I with her have spent.
Not Hermia but Helena I love:

115-21. Lysander, perhaps secretly worried by his own inconstancy, tries to argue that *reason* has caused him to change. In fact, he's never been so unreasonable as now when he's in the power of the magic drug.

115. 'Human reason controls desire (*will*).'

117. *their season:* the proper time of year.

118-20. 'My young brain has only just come to maturity, but now my intelligence (*skill*) is fully grown, reason takes command (*becomes the marshal*) of desire.' Lysander is trying to argue that when he loved Hermia he wasn't old enough to decide reasonably. Now that he is, he chooses Helena! (lines 121-2).

121. *o'erlook:* read.

123. Helena takes Lysander's compliments for cruel teasing – she thinks he's jeering at her as an unattractive girl who's born to be an old maid.

128. *flout my insufficiency:* 'make fun of my inadequacy'.

129. Breathless with misery and anger, she almost swears at him.

132. 'I thought you were more of a gentleman.'

133. *of:* by.

134. *abus'd:* wronged.

135. Hermia, of course, is lying as far off as she could get.

137-8. 'Just as too much (*a surfeit*) of the nicest food makes you sickest.'

139. 'Or as anyone who's held a false belief (*heresy*) hates it most when he's given it up.'

142. *Of:* by. Why do you think Lysander turns with such extreme violence against Hermia?

143. *address:* direct.

Who will not change a raven for a dove?
The will of man is by his reason sway'd,   *115*
And reason says you are the worthier maid.
Things growing are not ripe until their season;
So I, being young, till now ripe not to reason;
And touching now the point of human skill,
Reason becomes the marshal to my will,   *120*
And leads me to your eyes, where I o'erlook
Love's stories, written in Love's richest book.

Helena

Wherefore was I to this keen mockery born?
When at your hands did I deserve this scorn?
Is't not enough, is't not enough, young man,   *125*
That I did never, no, nor never can,
Deserve a sweet look from Demetrius' eye,
But you must flout my insufficiency?
Good troth, you do me wrong, good sooth, you do,
In such disdainful manner me to woo.   *130*
But fare you well; perforce I must confess
I thought you lord of more true gentleness.
O, that a lady of one man refus'd
Should of another therefore be abus'd!

Exit

Lysander

She sees not Hermia. Hermia, sleep thou there;   *135*
And never mayst thou come Lysander near!
For, as a surfeit of the sweetest things
The deepest loathing to the stomach brings,
Or as the heresies that men do leave
Are hated most of those they did deceive,   *140*
So thou, my surfeit and my heresy,
Of all be hated, but the most of me!
And, all my powers, address your love and might
To honour Helen, and to be her knight!

Exit

Stage Direction: Hermia, dreaming of Lysander's unkindness and treachery (symbolized by the snake), wakes from the nightmare to find him gone.

146. *serpent:* snake.

148. *quake:* shake.

150. *prey:* preying on me, eating me.

151. *remov'd?:* 'have you gone?'

153. *an if:* if only.

154. *of all loves:* 'in love's name!' *swoon:* faint.

155. *nigh:* near.

156. Lysander's loss is like death to Hermia, and she feels she must find him or die.

Hermia [*Starting*]

Help me, Lysander, help me; do thy best   145
To pluck this crawling serpent from my breast.
Ay me, for pity! What a dream was here!
Lysander, look how I do quake with fear.
Methought a serpent eat my heart away,
And you sat smiling at his cruel prey.   150
Lysander! What, remov'd? Lysander! lord!
What, out of hearing gone? No sound, no word?
Alack, where are you? Speak, an if you hear;
Speak, of all loves! I swoon almost with fear.
No? Then I well perceive you are not nigh.   155
Either death or you I'll find immediately.

Exit

ACT THREE

SCENE I

Now the players, the last of the humans to arrive in the magic wood, keep their appointment to rehearse, but when Puck takes a hand they're transformed into confused and unwilling actors in *his* entertainment. They see themselves in noble romantic parts, but Puck shows them up as the Fools they are by giving Bottom an ass's head and frightening the rest out of such sense as they possess.

2. *Pat, pat:* right to the minute.

3. *green plot:* grass lawn.

4. *hawthorn brake:* clump of hawthorn bushes. *tiring-house:* dressing-room.

6-64. Bottom having read the play is now full of well-meant criticism, and starts off a general discussion. The players, who seem to have the greatest difficulty telling the play and life apart, have two fears, one that it will be too real, the other that it won't be real enough. In their efforts to set things right everything fearful or romantic – the death of Pyramus, the Lion, the moon – gets turned to glorious comedy.

7. *bully Bottom:* 'Bottom, man!'

10. *the ladies* have to be specially considered in a wedding entertainment. One's an Amazon warrior, and the other two at this moment boldly adventuring in this very wood – but to Bottom and company they stand for all that's timid, delicate and refined.

12. *By'r lakin:* 'By our little Lady' (the Virgin Mary). *parlous:* 'awful' (a short form of 'perilous').

15. *Not a whit:* 'Not a bit of it'. Bottom delights in his ingenuity in overcoming a difficulty he himself has raised.

16. *prologue:* introduction.

18. *not kill'd indeed:* not really killed. This point is made again in the actual performance when Bottom jumps up after his 'death' (Act V, Scene i, line 337). *MND* is a comedy and though Shakespeare brings death into it with the Pyramus and Thisby play he's careful to rub in that it's all pretence – a comic tragedy. *for the more better assurance:* to make things even safer.

ACT THREE

SCENE I—*The wood.* TITANIA *lying asleep*

Enter QUINCE, SNUG, BOTTOM, FLUTE, SNOUT
and STARVELING

Bottom
> Are we all met?

Quince
> Pat, pat; and here's a marvellous convenient place for
> our rehearsal. This green plot shall be our stage, this
> hawthorn brake our tiring-house; and we will do it in
> action, as we will do it before the Duke. 5

Bottom
> Peter Quince!

Quince
> What sayest thou, bully Bottom?

Bottom
> There are things in this comedy of Pyramus and
> Thisby that will never please. First, Pyramus must
> draw a sword to kill himself; which the ladies cannot 10
> abide. How answer you that?

Snout
> By'r lakin, a parlous fear.

Starveling
> I believe we must leave the killing out, when all is
> done.

Bottom
> Not a whit; I have a device to make all well. Write 15
> me a prologue; and let the prologue seem to say we
> will do no harm with our swords, and that Pyramus
> is not kill'd indeed; and for the more better assurance,

19. *I Pyramus am not Pyramus.* Bottom seriously supposes the audience will think the characters are real, and mistake the play for life.
20. *put them out of fear:* stop them being afraid.

22. *eight and six:* a ballad metre with eight syllables (four beats) in one line and six (three beats) in the next, e.g.:

There lived a wife at Ushers well,

And a wealthy wife was she;

She had three stout and stalwart sons,

And sent them o'er the sea.

23-4. Bottom, who can never have too much of a good thing, wants eight syllables (four beats) in every line.
26. *I promise you:* 'I can tell you'.
27. *consider with yourself:* 'ask yourselves'.

29-30. *wildfowl:* wild animal. Bottom doesn't mean lions have wings, but that's the effect.
30. *look to't:* 'see to it'.

32-3. Like Bottom with the ass's head. Snug ends up a kind of comic monster, half a beast and half a man – which is suitable, since the foolish players have no more brains than beasts.
34. *defect:* effect.

38. *it were pity of my life:* 'it would be a sorry thing for me'.

43. Poetry creates the moonlight in *MND*, but Quince has no idea that his play should appeal to the imagination – he wants a real moon. Shakespeare gets in some subtle self-advertisement here, that is he is suggesting the importance of his own imaginative method.

tell them that I Pyramus am not Pyramus but Bottom
the weaver. This will put them out of fear.   20

Quince

Well, we will have such a prologue; and it shall be
written in eight and six.

Bottom

No, make it two more; let it be written in eight and
eight.

Snout

Will not the ladies be afeard of the lion?   25

Starveling

I fear it, I promise you.

Bottom

Masters, you ought to consider with yourself to bring
in—God shield us!—a lion among ladies is a most
dreadful thing; for there is not a more fearful wildfowl than your lion living; and we ought to look to't.   30

Snout

Therefore another prologue must tell he is not a lion.

Bottom

Nay, you must name his name, and half his face must
be seen through the lion's neck; and he himself must
speak through, saying thus, or to the same defect:
'Ladies,' or 'Fair ladies, I would wish you' or 'I would   35
request you' or 'I would entreat you not to fear, not
to tremble. My life for yours! If you think I come
hither as a lion, it were pity of my life. No, I am no
such thing; I am a man as other men are.' And there,
indeed, let him name his name, and tell them plainly   40
he is Snug the joiner.

Quince

Well, it shall be so. But there is two hard things—
that is, to bring the moonlight into a chamber; for,
you know, Pyramus and Thisby meet by moonlight.

Snout

Doth the moon shine that night we play our play?   45

93

46. *almanack:* a book of tables giving astronomical and astrological information for the year.

48. In fact the new moon would set just after sunset and before the time of the performance.

49. *casement:* the part of a window that opens.

52. *bush of thorns.* The man in the moon traditionally carried a bundle of thorns or sticks. He also had a dog (who appears in Act V, Scene i, line 250). The lantern, of course, stands for the moon itself.
53. Though Quince means 'figure' (stand for), *disfigure* ('make a guy of') may still be the better word!

57. *chink:* crack.

59. Notice how they all turn to Bottom as leader.

60. Living *Wall* is an even queerer creature than human *Lion.*

61. *loam . . . rough cast:* different kinds of plaster for walls. Loam was made of damp clay, sand, dung and straw; rough-cast was a mixture of lime and gravel.
63. *thus.* Bottom makes a sign with his open fingers. *cranny:* crack.

68. *brake:* the hawthorn bushes near them. *cue:* turn.

69. *hempen homespuns:* men with rough home-made clothes and manners. *swagg'ring:* showing-off. The sound of the line suggests their clumsy excited movements.

70. *cradle.* This word for bed makes us feel how delicate the fairies are compared with the big rough mortals. It's this contrast that makes Titania's love for Bottom (with a donkey's head as well) grotesquely funny.
71. 'What, they're getting up a play, are they?' *auditor:* listener.

Bottom
　A calendar, a calendar! Look in the almanack; find
out moonshine, find out moonshine.

Quince
　Yes, it doth shine that night.

Bottom
　Why, then may you leave a casement of the great
chamber window, where we play, open; and the　*50*
moon may shine in at the casement.

Quince
　Ay; or else one must come in with a bush of thorns
and a lantern, and say he comes to disfigure or to
present the person of Moonshine. Then there is
another thing: we must have a wall in the great　*55*
chamber; for Pyramus and Thisby, says the story, did
talk through the chink of a wall.

Snout
　You can never bring in a wall.
What say you, Bottom?

Bottom
　Some man or other must present Wall; and let him　*60*
have some plaster, or some loam, or some rough-cast
about him, to signify wall; and let him hold his fingers
thus, and through that cranny shall Pyramus and
Thisby whisper.

Quince
　If that may be, then all is well. Come, sit down, every　*65*
mother's son, and rehearse your parts. Pyramus, you
begin; when you have spoken your speech, enter into
that brake; and so every one according to his cue.

Enter PUCK *behind*

Puck
　What hempen homespuns have we swagg'ring here,
So near the cradle of the Fairy Queen?　　　　　*70*
What, a play toward! I'll be an auditor;
An actor too perhaps, if I see cause.

74. The rehearsal gets under way (these speeches of course aren't repeated when the play is acted in Act Five). Quince's poetry ridiculously exaggerates the faults of bad Elizabethan verse plays – artificial word patterns (87) and repetitions (77, 88), high-flown unlikely images, old-fashioned or invented 'poetic' words (87), together with almost total lack of sense. (Pyramus can't be red and white at once, he isn't a Jew, and the lovers' admiring descriptions of each other have nothing to do with what's happening.) But it has a certain vim; the *red rose on triumphant brier* is splendid. The verse should be spoken energetically but flatly, to give the impression that Bottom and Flute have even less idea what it means than the author, Quince.

74-6. Quince as producer tries to correct Bottom, without much success. *odious:* hateful; *odorous:* sweet-smelling; *odours:* smells.

80. Unheard and unseen by the actors, Puck finishes Bottom's speech for him – Bottom will *appear* as an extraordinary *Pyramus* when he returns with an ass's head.

87. *brisky juvenal:* lively youth. *eke:* also. *Jew:* short for 'juvenal', to rhyme with *hue* (85).

88-9. Flute forgets to pause at *never tire,* the signal for Bottom to enter.

89. *Ninny:* fool.

92. *cue:* the last few words at the end of a speech, the sign for the next speaker to come in.

Stage Direction: *Bottom with an ass's head.* The ass has two traditional associations, foolishness and sexual vigour. Shakespeare concentrates on Bottom's folly, and Puck gives him a visible ass-head because he has an invisible one already. But it's also the animal in him that appeals to Titania's rebellious sensuality, though this is no more than a suggestion, kept in the background. What is emphasized in his relationship with the fairy queen is the comic contrast between his vulgarity and Titania's aristocratic refinement.

Quince
  Speak, Pyramus. Thisby, stand forth.
Bottom
  Thisby, the flowers of odious savours sweet—
Quince
  'Odious'—odorous!   75
Bottom
  ——*odours savours sweet;*
  So hath thy breath, my dearest Thisby dear.
  But hark, a voice! Stay thou but here awhile,
  And by and by I will to thee appear.

                         Exit

Puck
  A stranger Pyramus than e'er played here!   80

                         Exit

Flute
  Must I speak now?
Quince
  Ay, marry, must you; for you must understand he
  goes but to see a noise that he heard, and is to come
  again.
Flute
  Most radiant Pyramus, most lily-white of hue,   85
  Of colour like the red rose on triumphant brier,
  Most brisky juvenal, and eke most lovely Jew,
  As true as truest horse, that yet would never tire,
  I'll meet thee, Pyramus, at Ninny's tomb.
Quince
  'Ninus' tomb,' man! Why, you must not speak that   90
  yet; that you answer to Pyramus. You speak all your
  part at once, cues and all. Pyramus enter: your cue is
  past; it is 'never tire.'
Flute
  O—*As true as truest horse, that yet would never tire.*

       Re-enter PUCK, *and* BOTTOM *with an ass's head*

95. Bottom, horribly transformed, muddles his punctuation, and changes 'If I were, fair Thisby' meaning 'If I were *true*', to *If I were fair, Thisby* . . . ('If I were really good-looking, I would be yours alone.')
96. *haunted*. Quince takes Bottom (who doesn't know what has happened and can't understand why they are all frightened) for an evil spirit.

98. 'I'll lead you a roundabout dance,' the kind of game Puck most enjoys (Act II, Scene i, lines 34-58). Unlike the round dances in which Titania leads her fairies, Puck's wild dance (or wild hunt) is one of confused disorder.
99. This line needs another word to make it scan, perhaps something like *Through bog, through brook.* . . .

104. *a knavery:* 'a trick they're playing'.

107. Bottom hints sarcastically that his friends are being silly asses. He has no idea he's wearing a donkey's head himself.

109. *translated:* transformed.

Bottom

    If I were fair, Thisby, I were only thine.   95

Quince

    O monstrous! O strange! We are haunted. Pray,
masters! fly, masters! Help!

Exeunt all but BOTTOM *and* PUCK

Puck

    I'll follow you; I'll lead you about a round,
Through bog, through bush, through brake, through
      brier;
Sometime a horse I'll be, sometime a hound,   *100*
A hog, a headless bear, sometime a fire;
And neigh, and bark, and grunt, and roar, and burn,
Like horse, hound, hog, bear, fire, at every turn.

Exit

Bottom

    Why do they run away? This is a knavery of them to
make me afeard.   *105*

Re-enter SNOUT

Snout

    O Bottom, thou art chang'd! What do I see on thee?

Bottom

    What do you see? You see an ass-head of your own,
do you?

Exit SNOUT
Re-enter QUINCE

Quince

    Bless thee, Bottom, bless thee! Thou art translated.

Exit

Bottom

    I see their knavery: this is to make an ass of me; to *110*
fright me, if they could. But I will not stir from this

115. *ousel cock:* blackbird.

116. *orange-tawny:* deep yellow.

117. *throstle:* thrush.

118. *little quill:* thin shrill song.

119. Bottom looks and sounds far from angelic: Titania in the grip of deluded passion (like Lysander, convinced her love is reasonable Act II, Scene ii, lines 115-22) stresses how spiritual her love is – Bottom's an angel, as wise as he is beautiful, and she plans to turn him into an *airy spirit* (149).

121. *plain-song:* a simple tune without variations, like the cuckoo's monotonous song.

122-3. 'Cuckoo!' was supposed to be a warning to husbands that their wives were unfaithful. The men in the song *dare not answer nay* because the warning is true – but Bottom of course misses the point.

124. *set his wit to:* argue with.

125. *give a bird the lie:* accuse a bird of lying.

128. *enamoured of:* delighted by.

129. *enthralled to:* held spellbound by.

130. 'The power of your excellence compels me.' But it's really the power of the love-juice that makes Titania love the half-animal, noisy, ugly, low-class, silly Bottom.

131. *On the first view.* Love in *MND* is at first sight, and strikes through the eyes.

132-3. Bottom is being politely modest, but he's quite right, Titania has little reason to love him. Though he's often ridiculous and doesn't understand what's going on, Bottom comes through his adventures with surprising common sense.

133-4. *reason and love keep little company together now-a-days.* Without knowing it Bottom puts his finger on what's wrong with all the lovers.

136. *gleek:* make a clever joke.

138. *Not so, neither:* 'indeed I'm not'. *wit:* sense.

139. *I have . . . turn:* 'it would be quite enough for me'.

place, do what they can; I will walk up and down
here, and I will sing, that they shall hear I am not
afraid.

Sings

> The ousel cock, so black of hue,   *115*
>   With orange-tawny bill,
> The throstle with his note so true,
>   The wren with little quill.

Titania

What angel wakes me from my flow'ry bed?

Bottom [Sings]

> The finch, the sparrow, and the lark,   *120*
>   The plain-song cuckoo grey,
> Whose note full many a man doth mark,
>   And dares not answer nay—

for, indeed, who would set his wit to so foolish a bird?
Who would give a bird the lie, though he cry 'cuckoo' *125*
never so?

Titania

I pray thee, gentle mortal, sing again.
Mine ear is much enamoured of thy note;
So is mine eye enthralled to thy shape;
And thy fair virtue's force perforce doth move me,   *130*
On the first view, to say, to swear, I love thee.

Bottom

Methinks, mistress, you should have little reason for
that. And yet, to say the truth, reason and love keep
little company together now-a-days. The more the
pity that some honest neighbours will not make them *135*
friends. Nay, I can gleek upon occasion.

Titania

Thou art as wise as thou art beautiful.

Bottom

Not so, neither; but if I had wit enough to get out of
this wood, I have enough to serve mine own turn.

141. Like other lovers Titania is selfish.

142. *common rate:* ordinary rank.

143. 'The summer always attends on my magnificence' (like a servant in the train of a great lady). Titania means that where she is it is always summer.

146. *the deep:* the sea.

148-9. 'I'll refine your solid human body till you move as a spirit' – Titania means to turn Bottom into a fairy.

150. Four tiny fairies with high-pitched voices answer.

153. *gambol:* leap about. The fairies are to jump and dance about where Bottom can see them.
154. *apricocks:* apricots. *dewberries* may be gooseberries, or else the fruit of the dwarf mulberry, which is still common round Stratford-on-Avon.

157. 'Chop off their wax-bearing thighs to make candles.'

158. The glow-worm's green light (which comes from the abdomen of the female, not the eye) would not really light a candle. Shakespeare's fairy world is both whimsical and cruel, as Titania's other orders show.
159. *To have my love to bed:* 'to show my love the way to bed'. *and to arise:* the fairies live in a dark world and generally avoid the morning.
160. *painted:* brightly coloured.

Titania

    Out of this wood do not desire to go;   *140*

    Thou shalt remain here whether thou wilt or no.

    I am a spirit of no common rate;

    The summer still doth tend upon my state;

    And I do love thee; therefore, go with me.

    I'll give thee fairies to attend on thee;   *145*

    And they shall fetch thee jewels from the deep,

    And sing, while thou on pressed flowers dost sleep;

    And I will purge thy mortal grossness so

    That thou shalt like an airy spirit go.

    Peaseblossom! Cobweb! Moth! and Mustardseed!   *150*

Enter PEASEBLOSSOM, COBWEB, MOTH,
and MUSTARDSEED

Peaseblossom

    Ready.

Cobweb   And I.

Moth   And I.

Mustardseed   And I.

All   Where shall we go?

Titania

    Be kind and courteous to this gentleman;

    Hop in his walks and gambol in his eyes;

    Feed him with apricocks and dewberries,

    With purple grapes, green figs, and mulberries;   *155*

    The honey bags steal from the humble-bees,

    And for night-tapers crop their waxen thighs,

    And light them at the fiery glow-worm's eyes,

    To have my love to bed and to arise;

    And pluck the wings from painted butterflies,   *160*

    To fan the moonbeams from his sleeping eyes.

    Nod to him, elves, and do him courtesies.

Peaseblossom

    Hail, mortal!

Cobweb

    Hail!

167. *I cry your worships mercy, heartily:* 'I'm much obliged to you, gentlemen.'

170. 'I look forward to knowing you better.'

171-2. Bottom, in Elizabethan fashion, would stop a cut with a cobweb (some English countrymen still do the same).

173. *Peaseblossom:* Pea-flower.

174-5. 'Give my regards to Mrs. Peapod – and to Mr. Peapod too.' *Squash:* young unripe peapod.

179-82. Bottom is teasing, since mustard is too hot for *patience*. Mustard plants (*many a gentleman of your house*) have fattened the beef which is afterwards eaten with mustard (*your kindred*) whose sad fate – or fiery taste – made Bottom cry. Bottom is very much at ease with the little fairies, and talks to them with friendly mock-politeness.

185. Titania interrupts Bottom before he can speak to the fourth fairy, *Moth* (the Elizabethan spelling of 'mote', a tiny speck of dust).
186-7. The moon looks misty and dew (supposed to come from it) is thick on the flowers.
189. Bottom, as usual, has been talking too much. His good-humoured vulgar chatter quite undoes the effect of Titania's elegant plans for his entertainment, and even in her enchanted state she feels it's better to keep him quiet. Bottom is led off in astonishment, trying to speak and failing.

Moth
Hail!   *165*
Mustardseed
Hail!
Bottom
I cry your worships mercy, heartily; I beseech your
worship's name.
Cobweb
Cobweb.
Bottom
I shall desire you of more acquaintance, good Master *170*
Cobweb. If I cut my finger, I shall make bold with
you. Your name, honest gentleman?
Peaseblossom
Peaseblossom.
Bottom
I pray you, commend me to Mistress Squash, your
mother, and to Master Peascod, your father. Good *175*
Master Peaseblossom, I shall desire you of more
acquaintance too. Your name, I beseech you, sir?
Mustardseed
Mustardseed.
Bottom
Good Master Mustardseed, I know your patience
well. That same cowardly giant-like ox-beef hath *180*
devour'd many a gentleman of your house. I promise
you your kindred hath made my eyes water ere now.
I desire you of more acquaintance, good Master
Mustardseed.
Titania
Come, wait upon him; lead him to my bower.   *185*
The moon, methinks, looks with a wat'ry eye;
And when she weeps, weeps every little flower,
Lamenting some enforced chastity.
Tie up my love's tongue, bring him silently.

Exeunt

105

SCENE II

This long scene is the climax of the lovers' adventures in the wood. Their relationships become finally and hopelessly entangled and they all begin to fight. It is Oberon who prevents bloodshed, and finally straightens out the knot when at the end they collapse in exhausted sleep.

The slow opening, with Puck reporting to Oberon, is designed to make sure the audience knows what's going on. (i) Titania is in love with Bottom: that plot's going well. (ii) An Athenian's eyes have been treated with the love-juice – *that is finish'd too* (38). But of course it was the wrong Athenian (Lysander instead of Demetrius, who is still after Hermia). Oberon at once starts to put things right by sending Puck for Helena while he himself anoints the eyes of Demetrius (94-9). But there's still plenty of comic confusion to follow, with Demetrius and Lysander now both wooing Helena while Hermia attacks her (282).

Though the final quarrel has serious, even tragic, undertones (only Oberon's intervention stops the men killing each other), the lovers' deadly earnestness only makes them funnier for the onlookers. The scene should be played as near-farce, at top speed, with exaggerated speech and gestures.

2. *what . . . next came in her eye:* what she saw next.

3. *dote on in extremity:* be utterly infatuated with.

4. *mad:* wild. Perhaps Puck dances or cartwheels in; and he enjoys wild confusion better than reasonable behaviour.

5. *night-rule:* night-time games and goings-on in the wood haunted by the fairies.

7. *close and consecrated:* private and holy.

8. *dull:* heavy with sleep.

9. *crew of patches:* gang of fools. Professional Elizabethan fools wore gaily patched clothes, and the Athenian players' working clothes may be in patches too. *rude mechanicals:* rough workmen.

10. *bread:* food, 'a living'.

13-14. 'The silliest of the stupid lot', Bottom, presented (*acted*) Pyramus. *sport:* play.

15. *Forsook his scene:* left the stage.

16. 'When I got this chance.'

17. *nole:* head.

18. *Anon:* soon.

19. *mimic:* comic actor. Puck is not impressed by Bottom's efforts to act tragically.

19-24. Puck compares the bird-witted players to hunted birds in a panic. (Animal imagery underlines the likeness between the Fools and the Lovers.)

20. 'Like wild geese who see the hunter creeping up.'

21. 'Or grey-headed jackdaws in a big flock.' *Chough* was another name for jackdaw in Shakespeare's time, and *russet*, which now means reddish brown, could then mean ash-grey.

22. *report:* bang.

SCENE II—*Another part of the wood*

Enter OBERON

Oberon
    I wonder if Titania be awak'd;
    Then, what it was that next came in her eye,
    Which she must dote on in extremity.

Enter PUCK

    Here comes my messenger. How now, mad spirit!
    What night-rule now about this haunted grove?   *5*
Puck
    My mistress with a monster is in love.
    Near to her close and consecrated bower,
    While she was in her dull and sleeping hour,
    A crew of patches, rude mechanicals,
    That work for bread upon Athenian stalls,   *10*
    Were met together to rehearse a play
    Intended for great Theseus' nuptial day.
    The shallowest thickskin of that barren sort,
    Who Pyramus presented, in their sport
    Forsook his scene and enter'd in a brake;   *15*
    When I did him at this advantage take,
    An ass's nole I fixed on his head.
    Anon his Thisby must be answered,
    And forth my mimic comes. When they him spy,
    As wild geese that the creeping fowler eye,   *20*
    Or russet-pated choughs, many in sort,
    Rising and cawing at the gun's report,

23. 'Split up and fly wildly in all directions.'

25. It is not clear why one of the players should fall over when Puck stamps, or why he says *our stamp*. Shakespeare may have written *a stump*, that is a tree-stump which the poor player tripped on.
27-8. 'Terror made them lose their silly heads and hurt themselves on everything.' Puck's victims, off their heads (*distracted*, line 31) with fright, lost such wits as they ever had.

29. *apparel:* clothes.

30. *from yielders all things catch:* 'everything steals from those who let go'.

32. *translated:* transformed.
35. 'This has worked better than I could have planned it.' The half-human, half-animal monster is odder than anything Oberon wished for Titania (Act II, Scene i, lines 180-1, Act II, Scene ii, lines 30-1) and makes a suitable punishment. But on the other hand Titania loving Bottom isn't seriously disgusting as it would be if she loved a real wild animal, and so her infatuation isn't out of key with *MND* as a comedy.
36. *latch'd:* wetted.

40. 'He was bound to see her when he woke up.' At this moment Demetrius and Hermia enter and Puck discovers his mistake. As we know, and Oberon soon guesses, he has accidentally charmed Lysander instead of Demetrius.

41. *close:* hidden (a reminder to the audience that the lovers don't see the fairies).

44. *Lay breath so bitter on:* speak so bitterly to. Demetrius, having at last found Hermia, is getting the same treatment he handed out to Helena in Act II, Scene i.
45. *chide:* scold. Hermia is more aggressive than Helena.

47. Hermia has an irrational fear Lysander must be dead, and pins it on Demetrius. The sense that death is always lying in wait for love becomes acute when the lovers are separated in the dark wood.
48. 'As you're already ankle-deep in blood, dive right in.'

Sever themselves and madly sweep the sky,
So at his sight away his fellows fly;
And at our stamp here, o'er and o'er one falls;   25
He murder cries, and help from Athens calls.
Their sense thus weak, lost with their fears thus strong,
Made senseless things begin to do them wrong,
For briers and thorns at their apparel snatch;
Some sleeves, some hats, from yielders all things
    catch.   30
I led them on in this distracted fear,
And left sweet Pyramus translated there;
When in that moment, so it came to pass,
Titania wak'd, and straightway lov'd an ass.

Oberon
This falls out better than I could devise.   35
But hast thou yet latch'd the Athenian's eyes
With the love-juice, as I did bid thee do?

Puck
I took him sleeping—that is finish'd too—
And the Athenian woman by his side;
That, when he wak'd, of force she must be ey'd.   40

     Enter DEMETRIUS *and* HERMIA

Oberon
Stand close; this is the same Athenian.

Puck
This is the woman, but not this the man.

Demetrius
O, why rebuke you him that loves you so?
Lay breath so bitter on your bitter foe.

Hermia
Now I but chide, but I should use thee worse,   45
For thou, I fear, hast given me cause to curse.
If thou hast slain Lysander in his sleep,
Being o'er shoes in blood, plunge in the deep,
And kill me too.
The sun was not so true unto the day   50

53. *whole:* solid. *bor'd:* pierced.

53-5. '. . . and that the moon could crawl through the middle of the earth to disturb the sun's (*Her brother's*) shining at midday for the people living on the other side (*th' Antipodes*).' Hermia can no more believe Lysander would desert her than that the moon and the sun could shine in the sky together – it's impossible, against the order of nature.

56. *It cannot be but thou hast:* 'you must have'.

57. *dead:* deadly pale.

58. Demetrius, who naturally doesn't care where Lysander has gone, turns the conversation back to himself, white as a corpse since Hermia 'murders' him by her disdain.

61. *Venus:* the evening star, planet of the goddess of love. *glimmering:* softly shining. The moon has set by now and this scene is acted by starlight – the wood gets darker, as the lovers' misunderstandings draw to a head.

62. 'What's that got to do with my Lysander?' Demetrius' complaints and compliments only annoy the anxious Hermia.

64. *carcass:* dead body.

65. *Out:* 'Shame on you!'; *cur:* dog (animal imagery again).

66. Hermia now fears Demetrius really *has* killed Lysander.

67. A murderer is an outcast.

69. 'You wouldn't have dared to stand up to him when he was awake, would you?'

70. *O brave touch!* 'a bold deed!'.

71. *worm:* snake.

72. *doubler:* more treacherous. But it's her Lysander who's the treacherous snake.

74. 'You're wasting your emotion in mistaken anger.'

76. 'He may not be dead, for all I know.'

78. 'What should I get for it if I could?'

79. 'The right never to see me again' – a right she means to give him anyway, and so she runs away (again treating him just as he treated Helena).

As he to me. Would he have stolen away
From sleeping Hermia? I'll believe as soon
This whole earth may be bor'd, and that the moon
May through the centre creep and so displease
Her brother's noontide with th' Antipodes.　　　55
It cannot be but thou hast murder'd him;
So should a murderer look—so dead, so grim.

Demetrius

So should the murdered look; and so should I,
Pierc'd through the heart with your stern cruelty;
Yet you, the murderer, look as bright, as clear,　　　60
As yonder Venus in her glimmering sphere.

Hermia

What's this to my Lysander? Where is he?
Ah, good Demetrius, wilt thou give him me?

Demetrius

I had rather give his carcass to my hounds.

Hermia

Out, dog! out, cur! Thou driv'st me past the bounds　　65
Of maiden's patience. Hast thou slain him, then?
Henceforth be never number'd among men!
O, once tell true; tell true, even for my sake!
Durst thou have look'd upon him being awake,
And hast thou kill'd him sleeping? O brave touch!　　70
Could not a worm, an adder, do so much?
An adder did it; for with doubler tongue
Than thine, thou serpent, never adder stung.

Demetrius

You spend your passion on a mispris'd mood:
I am not guilty of Lysander's blood;　　　75
Nor is he dead, for aught that I can tell.

Hermia

I pray thee, tell me then that he is well.

Demetrius

An if I could, what should I get therefore?

Hermia

A privilege never to see me more.

82. *vein:* mood.

84-7. A complicated way of saying 'sorrow grows worse for lack of sleep'. (Clearly, elaborate speech comes naturally to the sophisticated lovers – they don't just put it on to talk to each other.) *heaviness:* 'sadness' and also 'sleepiness'. Demetrius imagines *sleep* owes *sorrow* money, but is *bankrupt* (unable to pay) while he stays awake. But sleep will pay a little (*in some slight measure*) if he lies down to wait for its offer (*If for his tender here I make some stay*).

90-1. 'It's bound to follow from your mistake that a faithful lover will turn false, instead of a false lover turning faithful.'

92. 'Then fate takes charge and decides that, for one man who stays faithful, a million will fail, breaking promise after promise.' Puck revelling in the confusion pretends it's fate's fault, not his. But it's true that unfaithfulness does come naturally to lovers (Act I, Scene i, lines 238-41) – and that events nearly get out of Oberon's control.

96. *fancy-sick:* love-sick. *pale of cheer:* white-faced.

97. Elizabethans believed you lost a drop of blood every time you sighed.
98. *illusion:* deception, trick.
99. *against she do appear:* 'to be ready for when she comes'.

101. *Tartar's bow.* Eastern bows were very powerful and shot fast and hard. Puck shoots off-stage.

104. *apple:* pupil.

And from thy hated presence part I so;   80
See me no more whether he be dead or no.

Exit

Demetrius
There is no following her in this fierce vein;
Here, therefore, for a while I will remain.
So sorrow's heaviness doth heavier grow
For debt that bankrupt sleep doth sorrow owe;   85
Which now in some slight measure it will pay,
If for his tender here I make some stay.

Lies down

Oberon
What hast thou done? Thou hast mistaken quite,
And laid the love-juice on some true-love's sight.
Of thy misprision must perforce ensue   90
Some true love turn'd, and not a false turn'd true.

Puck
Then fate o'er-rules, that, one man holding troth,
A million fail, confounding oath on oath.

Oberon
About the wood go swifter than the wind,
And Helena of Athens look thou find;   95
All fancy-sick she is and pale of cheer,
With sighs of love that costs the fresh blood dear.
By some illusion see thou bring her here;
I'll charm his eyes against she do appear.

Puck
I go, I go; look how I go,   100
Swifter than arrow from the Tartar's bow.

Exit

Oberon
Flower of this purple dye,
Hit with Cupid's archery,
Sink in apple of his eye.

113

107. Helena must look like Love herself in Demetrius' eyes.

109. *remedy:* cure for love.

112. *the youth:* Lysander, whose eyes Puck anointed by mistake (Act II, Scene ii, line 78).

113. *fee:* a kiss, the lover's rightful reward.

114. *fond pageant:* silly performance. Puck has no sympathy with the lovers and enjoys their troubles like a play. The real audience can laugh too, since we know that in a comedy nothing can finally go wrong.

115. Puck lumps the actors in with the lovers as *fools.*

119. 'That's bound to be supremely funny.'

121. *befall prepost'rously:* turn out crazily.

122-33. For Lysander, the only truth is strong feeling – his tears prove he's sincere when he says he loves Helena. Helena, though she's a lover too, judges his behaviour reasonably from the outside. A man can't make the same vows to two women; either he's pretending to one for a joke, or he must be lying to both. This is an important exchange: up to now all the lovers have been acting out of irrational feeling, but now Helena shows she expects even love to make sense.

124-5. 'Their birth shows promises made in tears are genuine.'

126. *these things:* vows of love.

127. *the badge of faith:* his tears, a clear sign that he's speaking the truth.

128. *advance your cunning:* 'help on your trickery'. She thinks it's all a 'put-up job'.

129. Lysander's truth to Helena wipes out his truth to Hermia in a battle (*fray*) which is *holy* because between two truths, but devilish because they cancel each other out.

130. *give her o'er:* give her up, jilt her.

131-3. Weigh Lysander's vows to both women against each other and they balance out as equally worthless. Hermia opposes Lysander's appeal to emotion with an arithmetical and legal argument – Justice weighs the truth in a pair of scales. *even:* evenly. *tales:* lies.

When his love he doth espy,   *105*
Let her shine as gloriously
As the Venus of the sky.
When thou wak'st, if she be by,
Beg of her for remedy.

Re-enter PUCK

Puck

Captain of our fairy band,   *110*
Helena is here at hand,
And the youth mistook by me
Pleading for a lover's fee;
Shall we their fond pageant see?
Lord, what fools these mortals be!   *115*

Oberon

Stand aside. The noise they make
Will cause Demetrius to awake.

Puck

Then will two at once woo one.
That must needs be sport alone;
And those things do best please me   *120*
That befall prepost'rously.

Enter LYSANDER *and* HELENA

Lysander

Why should you think that I should woo in scorn?
Scorn and derision never come in tears.
Look when I vow, I weep; and vows so born,
In their nativity all truth appears.   *125*
How can these things in me seem scorn to you,
Bearing the badge of faith, to prove them true?

Helena

You do advance your cunning more and more.
When truth kills truth, O devilish-holy fray!
These vows are Hermia's. Will you give her o'er?   *130*
Weigh oath with oath, and you will nothing weigh:
Your vows to her and me, put in two scales,

134-5. Lysander still deceives himself with his original argument that his love for Hermia wasn't based on true reason and so he's acting reasonably now. But Helena sees through this.

136-7. A moment of pure farce – Demetrius' words and fervent tone flatly contradict Lysander.

137-44. Infatuation makes Demetrius exaggerate Helena's perfections out of all reason.

138. *eyne:* eyes.

139. *ripe in show:* ripe-looking.

141. *congealed:* frozen. *Taurus:* a mountain range in Turkey.

142. *Fann'd:* blown. *turns to a crow:* turns black (compared with her white hand).

144. *princess of pure white:* her hand, the *seal of bliss* because freely given it would confirm her lover's happiness – but she snatches it away.

145. *O spite! O hell!* Helena reacts to what she thinks Demetrius *really* means, which is hateful mockery.

145-6. 'I see you've made up your minds to set on me for fun.'

147. *civil:* not barbarians.

148. *injury:* insult.

149 and 154. *hate me, as I know you do . . . I am sure you hate me with your hearts.* Throughout the quarrel all four lovers ignore what the others actually say and respond to what they *know* (from past experience) they must mean. The result is that words no longer mean anything and they can't get through to each other at all.

150. *join in souls:* combine wholeheartedly.

151. *in show:* to look at.

153. *superpraise my parts:* praise my good points extravagantly.

157. *trim exploit:* 'pretty piece of work'. Helena is heavily sarcastic. *enterprise:* undertaking.

158. *conjure:* call.

159. *sort:* nature.

160. *extort:* torture.

162-76. Though their own hearts have changed, neither man will believe that the other now really loves Helena instead of Hermia.

162. Lysander, too, thinks Demetrius' sincere declaration of love for Helena must be unkind teasing.

163. *This you know I know:* but he doesn't; none of them knows what the others really feel.

Will even weigh; and both as light as tales.
Lysander
I had no judgment when to her I swore.
Helena
Nor none, in my mind, now you give her o'er.   *135*
Lysander
Demetrius loves her, and he loves not you.
Demetrius [*Awaking*]
O Helen, goddess, nymph, perfect, divine!
To what, my love, shall I compare thine eyne?
Crystal is muddy. O, how ripe in show
Thy lips, those kissing cherries, tempting grow!   *140*
That pure congealed white, high Taurus' snow,
Fann'd with the eastern wind, turns to a crow
When thou hold'st up thy hand. O, let me kiss
This princess of pure white, this seal of bliss!
Helena
O spite! O hell! I see you all are bent   *145*
To set against me for your merriment.
If you were civil and knew courtesy,
You would not do me thus much injury.
Can you not hate me, as I know you do,
But you must join in souls to mock me too?   *150*
If you were men, as men you are in show,
You would not use a gentle lady so:
To vow, and swear, and superpraise my parts,
When I am sure you hate me with your hearts.
You both are rivals, and love Hermia;   *155*
And now both rivals, to mock Helena.
A trim exploit, a manly enterprise,
To conjure tears up in a poor maid's eyes
With your derision! None of noble sort
Would so offend a virgin, and extort   *160*
A poor soul's patience, all to make you sport.
Lysander
You are unkind, Demetrius; be not so;
For you love Hermia. This you know I know;

164-7. He suggests they exchange girl-friends.

166. *bequeath:* leave.

168. Helena is convinced they're both acting. *idle breath:* useless talk.

169. *I will none:* 'I won't have her'.

171-2. 'My heart only visited Hermia, and now it's come back home to Helena.' In spite of the artificial-sounding praise he's been heaping on Helena, this turns out to be true. She is his old love, with whom he is at home.
173-5. The men begin to get heated.
174. *Disparage not:* 'don't run down'.

175. *aby it dear:* 'pay for it dearly'.

176. *dear:* darling, sweetheart. With Hermia's entry all four lovers are on stage together for the first time.

177-82. Hermia has found Lysander by his voice, since though you can't see in the dark you can hear twice as well.
177. *his function:* the eye's special power – seeing.
178. *more quick of apprehension:* keener.
179-80. 'Darkness pays hearing twice for having weakened sight.'

184-5. *love ... love.* Hermia thinks Lysander must mean his love for her, but of course he means his new love for Helena. Already they are talking at cross-purposes.

186. *bide:* stay.
187. *engilds:* brightens with golden light.
188. The stars, which Lysander points towards. *oes:* spangles, stars (i.e., round spots, like the letter 'o').
189. *this:* Helena's loveliness.
190. Suppressed guilt, as well as rage because she still claims him as her lover, makes Lysander hate Hermia.

And here, with all good will, with all my heart,
In Hermia's love I yield you up my part;   *165*
And yours of Helena to me bequeath,
Whom I do love and will do till my death.
Helena
Never did mockers waste more idle breath.
Demetrius
Lysander, keep thy Hermia; I will none.
If e'er I lov'd her, all that love is gone.   *170*
My heart to her but as guest-wise sojourn'd,
And now to Helen is it home return'd,
There to remain.   *Lysander*   Helen, it is not so.
Demetrius
Disparage not the faith thou dost not know,
Lest, to thy peril, thou aby it dear.   *175*
Look where thy love comes; yonder is thy dear.

Enter HERMIA

Hermia
Dark night, that from the eye his function takes,
The ear more quick of apprehension makes;
Wherein it doth impair the seeing sense,
It pays the hearing double recompense.   *180*
Thou art not by mine eye, Lysander, found;
Mine ear, I thank it, brought me to thy sound.
But why unkindly didst thou leave me so?
Lysander
Why should he stay whom love doth press to go?
Hermia
What love could press Lysander from my side?   *185*
Lysander
Lysander's love, that would not let him bide—
Fair Helena, who more engilds the night
Than all yon fiery oes and eyes of light.
Why seek'st thou me? Could not this make thee know
The hate I bare thee made me leave thee so?   *190*

191-2. Hermia can't believe Lysander means what he says, and at once Helena thinks she must be putting on an act.

192. *Lo:* 'see!' *confederacy:* conspiracy. Helena, shut up in her own miserable feelings of rejection and inferiority, decides they're all in the 'plot' to mock her by pretending to love her – not only the two men but Hermia egging them on.

193. *conjoin'd:* joined together.

194. 'To get up this treacherous game to spite me.'

195. *Injurious:* insulting.

197. *bait:* torment. Helena imagines herself as a helpless creature worried by savage dogs.

198-219. Helena, plaintively accusing, draws a sentimentally perfect picture of the two girls' childhood friendship. Notice how often she repeats *two, both* and *one* to make her point that they were *one* while seeming to be *two*. She excites herself by these repetitions till at the end her voice is full of tears.

198. *counsel:* confidences.

199. Helena and Hermia have always loved each other like sisters.

200-1. 'When we have scolded time for passing so quickly and separating us.'

203. *artificial gods:* skilful creators.

205. *sampler:* embroidery.

208. *incorporate:* belonging to one body.

209. *a double cherry:* two cherries with joined stalks.

211. *moulded:* formed.

212. 'Apparently with two bodies, but only one heart.'

213. *Two of the first:* 'two bodies', mentioned *first* in the line above (212). (*The first*, a heraldic term, means the first colour named in describing a coat of arms.)

213-14. Helena pictures their two bodies belonging to only one heart as a shield with two identical coats of arms on it, side by side, belonging to one person and beneath a single crest.

215. 'And will you tear up our old affection for each other?'

216. *join with:* side with.

217. *maidenly:* modest (i.e., the way a young girl should behave).

218. *Our sex:* women in general. *chide:* blame angrily.

220. *amazed.* Hermia has no notion what's biting Helena. She's still quite calm, more puzzled than annoyed.

Hermia

You speak not as you think; it cannot be.

Helena

Lo, she is one of this confederacy!
Now I perceive they have conjoin'd all three
To fashion this false sport in spite of me.
Injurious Hermia! most ungrateful maid!   *195*
Have you conspir'd, have you with these contriv'd,
To bait me with this foul derision?
Is all the counsel that we two have shar'd,
The sisters' vows, the hours that we have spent,
When we have chid the hasty-footed time   *200*
For parting us—O, is all forgot?
All school-days' friendship, childhood innocence?
We, Hermia, like two artificial gods,
Have with our needles created both one flower,
Both on one sampler, sitting on one cushion,   *205*
Both warbling of one song, both in one key;
As if our hands, our sides, voices, and minds,
Had been incorporate. So we grew together,
Like to a double cherry, seeming parted,
But yet an union in partition,   *210*
Two lovely berries moulded on one stem;
So, with two seeming bodies, but one heart;
Two of the first, like coats in heraldry,
Due but to one, and crowned with one crest.
And will you rent our ancient love asunder,   *215*
To join with men in scorning your poor friend?
It is not friendly, 'tis not maidenly;
Our sex, as well as I, may chide you for it,
Though I alone do feel the injury.

Hermia

I am amazed at your passionate words;   *220*
I scorn you not; it seems that you scorn me.

Helena

Have you not set Lysander, as in scorn,
To follow me and praise my eyes and face?

121

224. *your other love . . . :* all Helena's jealousy of Hermia is coming out
225. *even but now:* just now. *spurn me:* 'kick me away'.

227. *celestial.* heavenly. *Wherefore . . . ?*: why?

230. 'And offer (*tender*) affection to me, of all people!' (*forsooth* is a strongly sarcastic exclamation). Helena, bitterly ashamed because she can't attract a man and Hermia has two, thinks the others must be sneering at her total lack of sex-appeal.
231. *by your setting on:* 'because you put them up to it'. Her attack on Hermia is highly comic, considering both men now love her instead.
232. *in grace:* in favour.
234. *to love unlov'd:* 'loving someone who doesn't love me in return'.

236. This line might be a motto for the whole scene.

237. *Ay do:* she is still being sarcastic: *persever:* keep at it. *counterfeit sad looks:* 'keep your faces straight'.
238. *Make mouths upon me:* 'make faces at me'.
239. *hold the sweet jest up:* 'keep the rich joke going.'
240. 'This joke, if it comes off, can be put on record'.
241. *grace:* kindness.
242. *argument:* laughing-stock.
243. Why should it be partly Helena's own fault?
244. Because she's so miserable. As she starts to go, the men throw themselves in front of her begging her to stay. At this point the scene picks up pace and soon breaks up into frantic action and loud swearing.
245-8. This rapid exchange vividly shows up the lovers' total misunderstanding, as each responds in his or her own way – insulted (Helena), sweetly reproachful (Hermia), threatening (Demetrius) – to Lysander's 'joking', when he is in deadly earnest.

248. 'If Hermia can't persuade you to leave Helena alone, I can force you.'
251-5. Frustrated because Helena won't believe their vows of love, the two men challenge each other to fight. Since words aren't getting through, physical violence is the only way left to *prove* they mean what they say.
252. *that which I will lose for thee:* i.e., his life.

And made your other love, Demetrius,
Who even but now did spurn me with his foot,   225
To call me goddess, nymph, divine, and rare,
Precious, celestial? Wherefore speaks he this
To her he hates? And wherefore doth Lysander
Deny your love, so rich within his soul,
And tender me, forsooth, affection,   230
But by your setting on, by your consent?
What though I be not so in grace as you,
So hung upon with love, so fortunate,
But miserable most, to love unlov'd?
This you should pity rather than despise.   235

Hermia
I understand not what you mean by this.

Helena
Ay, do—persever, counterfeit sad looks,
Make mouths upon me when I turn my back,
Wink each at other; hold the sweet jest up;
This sport, well carried, shall be chronicled.   240
If you have any pity, grace, or manners,
You would not make me such an argument.
But fare ye well; 'tis partly my own fault,
Which death, or absence, soon shall remedy.

Lysander
Stay, gentle Helena; hear my excuse;   245
My love, my life, my soul, fair Helena!

Helena
O excellent!

Hermia   Sweet, do not scorn her so.

Demetrius
If she cannot entreat, I can compel.

Lysander
Thou canst compel no more than she entreat;
Thy threats have no more strength than her weak
     prayers.   250
Helen, I love thee, by my life I do;
I swear by that which I will lose for thee

123

255. 'Come away from the women and fight.'

256. Hermia hangs on to Lysander to make him notice her and stop him fighting.

257. *Ethiope:* Shakespeare uses this as an abusive term for a black person (Hermia is dark).
257-9. As Lysander struggles to break free from Hermia, Demetrius pretends to think he's taking cowardly advantage of her embrace to avoid fighting.
258. *take on as:* act as if.
259. *tame:* poor-spirited.
260-1. Demetrius called Helena *divine* (line 137), now Lysander calls Hermia *cat* and *serpent*. In the extremity of passion they no longer see each other as human at all. *Hang off:* 'let go!' *burr:* clinging prickly seed-box of a plant.
262. *rude:* uncivil, rough and unkind.

263. *Sweet love:* Hermia's slightly affected loving tones contrast comically with Lysander's swearing. Why is he so very rude to her?
263. *tawny Tartar:* dark brown gipsy, another term of abuse.
264. *med'cine:* poison. *potion:* drug.

265. Hermia, beginning to have doubts, clings to the 'joke' explanation. As Lysander forces her to see the truth (lines 269-81) the audience may become aware that it's not so funny after all. *sooth:* truly.

267-8. *bond:* binding written promise. *weak bond:* Hermia's arms (still chaining Lysander). *word:* word of honour.
269-70. Lysander is still controlled by something outside his own feelings – the code that forbids him to harm a woman. He speaks more angrily to Hermia in consequence.

272. *what news:* 'what's happened to make you hate me?'
273. But Lysander is no longer himself – he has lost contact with his own old self as well as with other people.
274. *erewhile:* a short time ago.

To prove him false that says I love thee not.
Demetrius
  I say I love thee more than he can do.
Lysander
  If thou say so, withdraw, and prove it too.   *255*
Demetrius
  Quick, come.
Hermia   Lysander, whereto tends all this?
Lysander
  Away, you Ethiope!
Demetrius   No, no, he will
  Seem to break loose—take on as you would follow,
  But yet come not. You are a tame man; go!
Lysander
  Hang off, thou cat, thou burr; vile thing, let loose,   *260*
  Or I will shake thee from me like a serpent.
Hermia
  Why are you grown so rude? What change is this,
  Sweet love?
Lysander   Thy love! Out, tawny Tartar, out!
  Out, loathed med'cine! O hated potion, hence!
Hermia
  Do you not jest?
Helena   Yes, sooth; and so do you.   *265*
Lysander
  Demetrius, I will keep my word with thee.
Demetrius
  I would I had your bond; for I perceive
  A weak bond holds you; I'll not trust your word.
Lysander
  What, should I hurt her, strike her, kill her dead?
  Although I hate her, I'll not harm her so.   *270*
Hermia
  What! Can you do me greater harm than hate?
  Hate me! wherefore? O me! what news, my love?
  Am not I Hermia? Are not you Lysander?
  I am as fair now as I was erewhile.

275. *since night:* to-night.

277. *In earnest.* She realizes the truth at last.
277-81. Lysander speaks as plainly and firmly as he can – there is a shocked silence.

282. The scene explodes into comedy again as Hermia turns violently on Helena. The pattern is reversed and *she* is now jealous of the successful woman for whom two men, including her own ex-lover, compete. *juggler:* cheat. *cankerblossom:* bud-eating maggot.

286. *bashfulness:* sensitive shrinking.

288. *Fie! fie!:* 'For shame!'; *counterfeit:* fake. *puppet:* little doll. She says that Hermia is too little and too wicked for a real human being.

291. *statures:* heights. *urg'd:* pleaded (as a point in her favour).

292. *personage:* figure. Now it's Hermia's turn to be sarcastic.

293. *prevail'd with him:* won him to love her.

294. 'Have you made him value you so highly . . .?'

295. *low:* short. Hermia advances on Helena and squints up into her face.

296. Helena is tall and slender with bright pink cheeks. *painted:* made up. On May-day holidaymakers danced round a tall brightly-painted maypole. The difference between their heights is grotesquely exaggerated as, calling each other dwarf and maypole, the tall girl retreats before the little one's attack.

298. As Hermia tries to scratch her, Helena backs away, trembling.

300. *curst:* bad-tempered.

301. *shrewishness:* spiteful scolding.

302. *right maid:* true girl (i.e., 'I know I'm a coward, but that's only feminine').

304. *something lower:* rather shorter.

305. *match her:* stand up to her in a fight.

Since night you lov'd me; yet since night you left me. *275*
Why then, you left me—O, the gods forbid!—
In earnest, shall I say?
Lysander   Ay, by my life!
And never did desire to see thee more.
Therefore be out of hope, of question, of doubt;
Be certain, nothing truer; 'tis no jest   *280*
That I do hate thee and love Helena.
Hermia
O me! you juggler! you cankerblossom!
You thief of love! What! Have you come by night,
And stol'n my love's heart from him?
Helena   Fine, i' faith!
Have you no modesty, no maiden shame,   *285*
No touch of bashfulness? What! Will you tear
Impatient answers from my gentle tongue?
Fie, fie! you counterfeit, you puppet you!
Hermia
'Puppet!' why so? Ay, that way goes the game.
Now I perceive that she hath made compare   *290*
Between our statures; she hath urg'd her height;
And with her personage, her tall personage,
Her height, forsooth, she hath prevail'd with him.
And are you grown so high in his esteem
Because I am so dwarfish and so low?   *295*
How low am I, thou painted maypole? Speak.
How low am I? I am not yet so low
But that my nails can reach unto thine eyes.
Helena
I pray you, though you mock me, gentlemen,
Let her not hurt me. I was never curst;   *300*
I have no gift at all in shrewishness;
I am a right maid for my cowardice;
Let her not strike me. You perhaps may think,
Because she is something lower than myself,
That I can match her.
Hermia   'Lower' hark, again.   *305*

306. Helena, sad over broken friendship as well as lost love, grows tearfully sorry for herself.

308. *counsels:* secrets.

310. *stealth:* secret escape.

312. *chid me hence:* driven me angrily away.
313. *spurn:* kick or push away.

315. Helena has always known that *folly* goes with love (Act I, Scene i, line 236).

317. *simple:* well-meaning. *fond:* silly and affectionate. Helena hopes to make them sorry for her by running herself down, but Hermia is not impressed.

323. *keen and shrewd:* fierce and malicious. Backed up by the men Helena becomes bolder.
324. *vixen:* female fox, proverbial for a shrewish woman – a comic contrast with her idealized description of their schooldays (lines 198-214).

327. *suffer her:* let her. *flout:* insult.
328. As Hermia goes for Helena again Lysander shoves her away.

329-30. *minimus:* pigmy. *hind'ring knot-grass:* a trailing weed that interferes with walking (as Hermia's arms have been hindering Lysander) and whose juice was supposed to stunt growth. *bead . . . acorn.* Lysander fantastically exaggerates the sneers at Hermia's smallness.
330. *Officious:* forward, interfering.
331. *In her behalf:* on her (Helena's) account.

Helena

 Good Hermia, do not be so bitter with me.
 I evermore did love you, Hermia,
 Did ever keep your counsels, never wrong'd you;
 Save that, in love unto Demetrius,
 I told him of your stealth unto this wood.   310
 He followed you; for love I followed him;
 But he hath chid me hence, and threaten'd me
 To strike me, spurn me, nay, to kill me too;
 And now, so you will let me quiet go,
 To Athens will I bear my folly back,   315
 And follow you no further. Let me go.
 You see how simple and how fond I am.

Hermia

 Why, get you gone! Who is't that hinders you?

Helena

 A foolish heart that I leave here behind.

Hermia

 What! with Lysander?

Helena   With Demetrius.   320

Lysander

 Be not afraid; she shall not harm thee, Helena.

Demetrius

 No, sir, she shall not, though you take her part.

Helena

 O, when she is angry, she is keen and shrewd;
 She was a vixen when she went to school;
 And, though she be but little, she is fierce.   325

Hermia

 'Little' again! Nothing but 'low' and 'little'!
 Why will you suffer her to flout me thus?
 Let me come to her.

Lysander   Get you gone, you dwarf;
 You minimus, of hind'ring knot-grass made;
 You bead, you acorn.

Demetrius   You are too officious   330
 In her behalf that scorns your services.

333. *intend:* offer.

335. *she:* i.e., Hermia.

336-7. 'To test which of us has most right to Helena.' Wrapped up in their quarrel the men take no notice of what Helena herself may feel. Love as a bridge between the sexes has broken right down – they've separated out into fighting pairs, man against man and woman against woman.

338. *cheek by jowl:* side by side.

339. *mistress:* miss, 'my fine lady'. *coil:* row. *long of you:* 'your fault'.

340. Helena again backs as Hermia comes on.

341. *curst:* vicious.

342. *fray:* fight.

343. *to run away*. She suits the action to the words.

344. *amaz'd:* utterly astonished and bewildered. Words having proved useless to discover what was happening, Hermia is reduced to silence.

345. Oberon steps forward to rebuke Puck for the lovers' disaster. *negligence:* carelessness. *Still thou mistak'st:* 'you make mistakes all the time'.

346. 'Or else you play your tricks deliberately.'

347. *shadows:* spirits.

348-51. Puck did exactly as he was told.

350-1. 'And, in so far as I did bathe an Athenian's eyes, I'm not to blame.'

352. *sort:* turn out.

353. *jangling:* squabbling. *sport:* amusement. Puck always regards the mortals as a show laid on for his benefit.

354-77. Now comes the last stage of the night's adventures, which only Oberon can bring to a happy conclusion for the lovers, and for Titania and himself. Though Puck can prevent them from killing each other, the lovers must still go through deadly despair and exhaustion before beginning a new and loving life at home in Athens: but when Titania's punishment too is ended *all things shall be peace* (line 377).

Let her alone; speak not of Helena;
Take not her part; for if thou dost intend
Never so little show of love to her,
Thou shalt aby it.

Lysander   Now she holds me not.   335
Now follow, if thou dar'st, to try whose right,
Of thine or mine, is most in Helena.

Demetrius
Follow! Nay, I'll go with thee, cheek by jowl.

Exeunt LYSANDER *and* DEMETRIUS

Hermia
You, mistress, all this coil is long of you.
Nay, go not back.

Helena   I will not trust you, I;   340
Nor longer stay in your curst company.
Your hands than mine are quicker for a fray;
My legs are longer though, to run away.

Exit

Hermia
I am amaz'd, and know not what to say.

Exit

Oberon
This is thy negligence. Still thou mistak'st,   345
Or else committ'st thy knaveries wilfully.

Puck
Believe me, king of shadows, I mistook.
Did not you tell me I should know the man
By the Athenian garments he had on?
And so far blameless proves my enterprise   350
That I have 'nointed an Athenian's eyes;
And so far am I glad it so did sort,
As this their jangling I esteem a sport.

Oberon
Thou seest these lovers seek a place to fight.

131

355. *hie:* hurry. *overcast:* cloud over.

356. *welkin:* sky.

357. *drooping:* low-lying. *Acheron:* the darkest river of Hell.

358. *testy:* angry and aggressive.

359. *as:* that. Oberon means to separate the rivals and prevent the fight.

360. *frame thy tongue:* speak.

362. *rail thou:* hurl insults.

364. *brows:* faces. *death-counterfeiting sleep:* 'sleep like death', from which the lovers will wake to a new life.

365. Oberon pictures sleep as a giant bat crawling over the lovers. *leaden:* dull and heavy. *batty:* bat-like.

366. *this herb:* another plant, which can undo the bad effects of the love-juice.

367. *virtuous property:* powerful quality.

368. *his might:* its (the juice's) power.

369. 'And make him see as usual.' Of course Demetrius must be left with enchanted eyes to go on loving Helena.

370. *derision:* ridiculous state of things.

371. The nightmare experience of the final quarrel when the lovers lost touch with reality was too confusing and horrible to be remembered clearly, and Oberon promises that it will *seem a dream*. *fruitless:* empty – it produced nothing but sterile hate, and it will fade away like a dream when the lovers wake up to real life again.

372. *back to Athens:* that is, back to everyday life and normal human society. *wend:* go.

373. *league:* alliance. Each pair of lovers will be permanently united, and all four will be friends. *date:* time of lasting.

375. Oberon quickly plans to wind up his quarrel with Titania by getting the changeling from her.

376-7. 'I'll set free her enchanted (*charmed*) eyes from concentrating on the monster.'

377. Unlike Puck, Oberon is ultimately on the side of order.

379-80. There's a sense of mounting urgency, for though the stage is dark and will grow darker when Puck calls up the enchanted fog, dawn is coming.

379. 'Night is passing swiftly.' *dragons.* Night's chariot is drawn by dragons that never sleep.

380. *Aurora's harbinger:* the morning star, forerunner of Aurora the dawn goddess.

381-7. Why, just before dawn and the healing of the lovers, does Puck suddenly remind us of death?

382. *troop:* go thronging. Ghosts had to be back in their graves before first light. *Damned spirits:* the ghosts of the damned. Suicides were considered damned and were buried at cross-roads without Christian ceremonies (except for those who drowned themselves and whose bodies were lost).

384. *wormy beds:* graves full of the worms that feed on decaying corpses.

386. *wilfully:* of their own accord. *exil'd:* shut out.

Hie therefore, Robin, overcast the night;   *355*
The starry welkin cover thou anon
With drooping fog as black as Acheron,
And lead these testy rivals so astray
As one come not within another's way.
Like to Lysander sometime frame thy tongue,   *360*
Then stir Demetrius up with bitter wrong;
And sometime rail thou like Demetrius;
And from each other look thou lead them thus,
Till o'er their brows death-counterfeiting sleep
With leaden legs and batty wings doth creep.   *365*
Then crush this herb into Lysander's eye;
Whose liquor hath this virtuous property,
To take from thence all error with his might
And make his eyeballs roll with wonted sight.
When they next wake, all this derision   *370*
Shall seem a dream and fruitless vision;
And back to Athens shall the lovers wend
With league whose date till death shall never end.
Whiles I in this affair do thee employ,
I'll to my queen, and beg her Indian boy;   *375*
And then I will her charmed eye release
From monster's view, and all things shall be peace.

Puck

My fairy lord, this must be done with haste,
For night's swift dragons cut the clouds full fast;
And yonder shines Aurora's harbinger,   *380*
At whose approach ghosts, wand'ring here and there,
Troop home to churchyards. Damned spirits all,
That in cross-ways and floods have burial,
Already to their wormy beds are gone,
For fear lest day should look their shames upon;   *385*
They wilfully themselves exil'd from light,

387. *consort with:* keep company with. *black-brow'd night:* Puck imagines night with a dark frowning face.

388. In spite of Puck's lawlessness, the fairies are good spirits. Oberon pushes back the thought of death with a sudden glow of light and colour as he describes the sunrise.

389. Literally, 'I've often made love with Aurora' but Oberon is probably speaking metaphorically, and simply means that he is not one of the spirits which are condemned to night-time activity only.

390. 'I may walk in the woods as a hunter.'

391. *the eastern gate:* the eastern horizon where the sun rises over the sea.

392. *Neptune:* the sea. *fair blessed beams* – of sunlight.

393. *streams:* waters. New life comes from the sea warmed by the sun, and seems to pour from Oberon's invigorating words.

394. *notwithstanding:* 'even though we aren't afraid of light'.

395. *effect this business:* 'finish this work'.

396. As Puck recites his favourite spell for leading wanderers astray black fog blots out the stars. The rest of the scene could be acted almost in darkness.

399. *Goblin:* Puck himself.

402. *drawn and ready:* with sword drawn and ready to fight.

403. *straight:* straightaway.

404. *plainer:* more even.

And must for aye consort with black-brow'd night.
Oberon
But we are spirits of another sort:
I with the Morning's love have oft made sport;
And, like a forester, the groves may tread   390
Even till the eastern gate, all fiery red,
Opening on Neptune with fair blessed beams,
Turns into yellow gold his salt green streams.
But, notwithstanding, haste, make no delay;
We may effect this business yet ere day.   395

Exit OBERON

Puck
      Up and down, up and down,
      I will lead them up and down.
      I am fear'd in field and town.
      Goblin, lead them up and down.
Here comes one.   400

Enter LYSANDER

Lysander
Where art thou, proud Demetrius? Speak thou now.
Puck
Here, villain, drawn and ready. Where art thou?
Lysander
I will be with thee straight.
Puck   Follow me, then,
To plainer ground.

Exit LYSANDER *as following the voice*
Enter DEMETRIUS

Demetrius
           Lysander, speak again.
Thou runaway, thou coward, art thou fled?   405

407. *bragging:* boasting.

408. 'Challenging the bushes to a fight.'

409. *recreant:* coward.

410. Elizabethan children were usually punished by beating.

410-11. *He is . . . thee:* 'It would be dishonourable to fight a baby like you with grown-up weapons'.

412. *try no manhood:* 'we won't test our courage'.

413. *still dares me on:* 'keeps daring me to follow'.

417. 'So I've come to rough ground where I can't see my way.' But the darkness and difficulty are also in Lysander's mind.

418-19. Each of the lovers falls asleep longing for morning.

419. *grey light.* Lysander doesn't expect a joyful dawn.

420. *spite:* injury.

421. *Ho, ho, ho!* Puck is enjoying himself.

422. *Abide me:* 'stop and wait for me'. *wot:* know.

423. *shifting:* changing.

425. Puck's voice comes from a distance and Demetrius despairs of catching up.

Speak! In some bush? Where dost thou hide thy
    head?

Puck

Thou coward, art thou bragging to the stars,
Telling the bushes that thou look'st for wars,
And wilt not come? Come, recreant, come, thou
    child;
I'll whip thee with a rod. He is defil'd   *410*
That draws a sword on thee.

Demetrius   Yea, art thou there?

Puck

Follow my voice; we'll try no manhood here.

Exeunt
Re-enter LYSANDER

Lysander

He goes before me, and still dares me on;
When I come where he calls, then he is gone.
The villain is much lighter heel'd than I.   *415*
I followed fast, but faster he did fly,
That fallen am I in dark uneven way,
And here will rest me. [*Lies down*] Come, thou gentle
    day.
For if but once thou show me thy grey light,
I'll find Demetrius, and revenge this spite.   *420*

Sleeps
Re-enter PUCK *and* DEMETRIUS

Puck

Ho, ho, ho! Coward, why com'st thou not?

Demetrius

Abide me, if thou dar'st; for well I wot
Thou runn'st before me, shifting every place,
And dar'st not stand, nor look me in the face.
Where art thou now?

Puck   Come hither; I am here.   *425*

137

426. *buy this dear:* 'you'll pay for this'.

428. *Faintness constraineth:* 'exhaustion forces'.

430. 'Be ready for an attack at dawn.'

432. *Abate:* shorten. *comforts:* i.e., the light and warmth of the rising sun.
433. *Athens.* Helena's one thought is to escape back to civilization.
434. *detest:* curse and hate.

436. *Steal me:* hide me.

437. Puck magically summons Hermia, so that, without knowing it, all four lovers fall asleep side by side.
438. *kinds:* sexes. Puck doesn't see the lovers as people but simply as males and females driven by impersonal desires.
439. *curst:* angry.
440. *knavish lad:* teasing boy.
441. *mad:* desperate.

443. *Bedabbled:* wet and muddied.

445. *can keep no pace with:* 'can't keep up with'.

447. *shield:* protect. *fray:* fight. Hermia's love for Lysander is unchanged by the horrible things he has said to her.

Demetrius

Nay, then, thou mock'st me. Thou shalt buy this
dear,
If ever I thy face by daylight see;
Now, go thy way. Faintness constraineth me
To measure out my length on this cold bed.
By day's approach look to be visited.   *430*

Lies down and sleeps
Enter HELENA

Helena

O weary night, O long and tedious night,
Abate thy hours! Shine comforts from the east,
That I may back to Athens by daylight,
From these that my poor company detest.
And sleep, that sometimes shuts up sorrow's eye,   *435*
Steal me awhile from mine own company.

Sleeps

Puck

Yet but three? Come one more;
Two of both kinds makes up four.
Here she comes, curst and sad.
Cupid is a knavish lad,   *440*
Thus to make poor females mad.

Enter HERMIA

Hermia

Never so weary, never so in woe,
Bedabbled with the dew, and torn with briers,
I can no further crawl, no further go;
My legs can keep no pace with my desires.   *445*
Here will I rest me till the break of day.
Heavens shield Lysander, if they mean a fray!

Lies down and sleeps

452. *Gentle lover*. Lysander hasn't always behaved very courteously, but Puck is restoring him to his true nature.

457. *former lady:* i.e., Hermia.
458. *proverb:* wise saying. *known:* 'that everybody knows'.

461. 'The right man will get the right girl.'
462. 'Nothing will go wrong.'

463. Another proverb meaning 'Everyone will get his own belongings back and everything will turn out right'. *mare:* female horse, and here perhaps 'woman'. Puck's last words, treating the lovers as natural and not very important, are comforting in their ordinariness.

Puck

> On the ground
> Sleep sound;
> I'll apply   *450*
> To your eye,
> Gentle lover, remedy.

[*Squeezing the juice on* LYSANDER'S *eyes*]

> When thou wak'st,
> Thou tak'st
> True delight   *455*
> In the sight
> Of thy former lady's eye;
> And the country proverb known,
> That every man should take his own,
> In your waking shall be shown: *460*
> Jack shall have Jill;
> Nought shall go ill;

The man shall have his mare again, and all shall be
    well.

Exit

ACT FOUR

SCENE I

In this scene, which falls into four parts (Bottom and Titania, lines 1-45; Oberon and Titania, lines 46-102; Theseus, Hippolyta and the lovers, lines 103-99; Bottom's awakening, lines 200-218), the night's adventures are happily wound up. Bottom and Titania are given one love-scene (1-45) before her infatuation ends, but Bottom's too busy getting the fairies to make him comfortable to attend to Titania, whose tender advances look silly in the light of his commonplace replies. Shakespeare deliberately plays down the sexual side of their relationship since he wants to keep it light and funny, and avoid disgust.

2. *amiable:* lovable. *coy:* stroke, caress. Titania strokes Bottom amorously – but he prefers a good scratch from the attendant fairies.

7. There's an amusing clash between Bottom's natural behaviour (when he itches, he scratches) and Titania's attempts to treat him as a refined and aristocratic lover. All his requirements are vulgarly physical – scratching, food, and sleep. *Mounsieur:* an old-fashioned spelling of 'Monsieur'. Bottom tries to be very polite.

11. *red-hipp'd:* with red thighs.
12. *humble-bee:* bumble bee.
13. *honey-bag:* the enlargement of the alimentary canal in which the bee carries its honey. *fret:* tire.
14. *action:* fight.

16. *loath:* sorry. *overflowen:* swamped by (another reminder of how tiny the fairies are).
17. *signior:* sir. Bottom, copying court-manners, switches to Italian.

142

ACT FOUR

SCENE I—*The wood* LYSANDER, DEMETRIUS, HELENA *and*
HERMIA, *lying asleep*

Enter TITANIA *and* BOTTOM; PEASEBLOSSOM, COBWEB,
MOTH, MUSTARDSEED *and other* FAIRIES *attending;*
OBERON *behind, unseen*

Titania
  Come, sit thee down upon this flow'ry bed,
  While I thy amiable cheeks do coy,
  And stick musk-roses in thy sleek smooth head,
  And kiss thy fair large ears, my gentle joy.
Bottom
  Where's Peaseblossom?   5
Peaseblossom
  Ready.
Bottom
  Scratch my head, Peaseblossom. Where's Mounsieur
  Cobweb?
Cobweb
  Ready.
Bottom
  Mounsieur Cobweb; good mounsieur, get you your   10
  weapons in your hand and kill me a red-hipp'd
  humble-bee on the top of a thistle; and, good
  mounsieur, bring me the honey-bag. Do not fret
  yourself too much in the action, mounsieur; and,
  good mounsieur, have a care the honey-bag break   15
  not; I would be loath to have you overflowen with a
  honey-bag, signior. Where's Mounsieur Mustardseed?

20. *neaf:* hand.

20-21. 'There's no need to keep bowing.' Bottom exchanging courtesies with a fairy the size of his finger nail is a ludicrous vision – it's a pity the actor must be at least child-sized.

23. *Cavalery:* probably Spanish 'Cavaliero' (gentleman). Bottom forgets that it's Peaseblossom who was to scratch.

25. Bottom has no idea what has happened to him.

26. *tender ass:* sensitive fool (with an unconscious pun).

29. *reasonable:* fairly.

29-30. *the tongs and the bones:* the clumsiest possible musical instruments, a pair of tongs struck with a metal key and two flat bones clapped together like castanets. The idea of this music is too much for Titania even in her infatuated state.

32. *a peck of provender:* heaps of food. *munch:* chew noisily.

33. *bottle:* bundle.

34. *fellow:* equal. Bottom has grown a donkey's appetite as well as a donkey's head.

35. *venturous:* adventurous, brave. The squirrel would fight to protect his hoard.

36. *hoard:* store.

39. *exposition of:* Bottom's mistake for 'disposition for' (desire for) sleep.

41. *be all ways away:* be off in all directions (to keep guard).

42-5. Titania fervently embraces Bottom, who's probably already snoring.

Mustardseed
  Ready.
Bottom
  Give me your neaf, Mounsieur Mustardseed. Pray   20
  you, leave your curtsy, good mounsieur.
Mustardseed
  What's your will?
Bottom
  Nothing, good mounsieur, but to help Cavalery
  Cobweb to scratch. I must to the barber's, mounsieur;
  for methinks I am marvellous hairy about the face;   25
  and I am such a tender ass, if my hair do but tickle
  me I must scratch.
Titania
  What, wilt thou hear some music, my sweet love?
Bottom
  I have a reasonable good ear in music. Let's have the
  tongs and the bones.   30
Titania
  Or say, sweet love, what thou desirest to eat.
Bottom
  Truly, a peck of provender; I could munch your good
  dry oats. Methinks I have a great desire to a bottle of
  hay. Good hay, sweet hay, hath no fellow.
Titania
  I have a venturous fairy that shall seek   35
  The squirrel's hoard, and fetch thee new nuts.
Bottom
  I had rather have a handful or two of dried peas. But,
  I pray you, let none of your people stir me; I have an
  exposition of sleep come upon me.
Titania
  Sleep thou, and I will wind thee in my arms.   40
  Fairies, be gone, and be all ways away.

Exeunt FAIRIES

42. *woodbine:* bindweed.

43. *entwist:* twist in with. *ivy* is *female* because it always needs something to cling to.

44. *Enrings:* circles round. *barky fingers:* twigs covered with bark.

46-102. Now that Oberon has won the child from Titania his anger against her is exhausted and he washes her eyes from the juice. Bottom loses the ass's head, and Oberon and Titania's dance of reconciliation rocks the lovers in a healing sleep, before the fairies, planning to return and bless the human marriages next night, fly off after the departing darkness.

46. *Robin:* Puck. *sweet sight:* Oberon is sarcastic.

47. *dotage:* infatuation.

48. *of late:* lately.

49. *sweet favours:* love-gifts of sweet-smelling flowers.

51. *temples:* forehead. *rounded:* encircled, crowned.

52. *coronet:* garland.

53. *sometime:* sometimes.

54. *Was wont to:* used to.

53-6. *orient pearls:* specially precious and brilliant Indian pearls. These 'pearls' of dew (like the cowslip's ear-drops, Act II, Scene i, line 15) are the flowers' jewellery, but those in the little flowers (*flowerets*) picked for Bottom were like tears of shame.

57. 'When I'd reproached her scornfully as much as I liked.' Perhaps an Elizabethan audience would have approved of Oberon's triumph over his wife, but he also has angry feelings to get out of his system before they can be friends again.

58. *mild terms:* gentle words.

59-60. Titania, too taken up with Bottom to care whether she kept the child or not, obeyed Oberon willingly.

64. *transformed scalp:* changed head-covering.

65. *swain:* lover (i.e., Bottom).

66. *other:* others.

67. *repair:* return.

68. *accidents:* unusual events.

69. *fierce vexation:* violent trouble. The Athenians will remember the night's doings as a nightmare that vanishes on waking.

So doth the woodbine the sweet honeysuckle
Gently entwist; the female ivy so
Enrings the barky fingers of the elm.
O, how I love thee! how I dote on thee!   45

They sleep
Enter PUCK

Oberon [*Advancing*]
Welcome, good Robin. Seest thou this sweet sight?
Her dotage now I do begin to pity;
For, meeting her of late behind the wood,
Seeking sweet favours for this hateful fool,
I did upbraid her and fall out with her.   50
For she his hairy temples then had rounded
With coronet of fresh and fragrant flowers;
And that same dew which sometime on the buds
Was wont to swell like round and orient pearls
Stood now within the pretty flowerets' eyes,   55
Like tears that did their own disgrace bewail.
When I had at my pleasure taunted her,
And she in mild terms begg'd my patience,
I then did ask of her her changeling child;
Which straight she gave me, and her fairy sent   60
To bear him to my bower in fairy land.
And now I have the boy, I will undo
This hateful imperfection of her eyes.
And, gentle Puck, take this transformed scalp
From off the head of this Athenian swain,   65
That he awaking when the other do
May all to Athens back again repair,
And think no more of this night's accidents
But as the fierce vexation of a dream.
But first I will release the Fairy Queen.   70

[*Touching her eyes*]

Be as thou wast wont to be;
See as thou wast wont to see.

73. *Dian's bud:* a flower belonging to Diana, goddess of chastity (see Act II, Scene i, line 184 and Act III, Scene ii, lines 366-9) whose juice can undo the effects of *Cupid's flower*, the flower of love (Act II, Scene i, lines 165-8).

76-7. Titania thinks she has dreamed her love for Bottom (as in a sense she has, since the reasonable part of her brain was no more in control when she loved him than in dreaming).

79. *visage:* face.

80-2. At Oberon's command Titania calls for music to cast Bottom and the four lovers into deeper, healing sleep. *common:* ordinary. *the sense:* the senses.

84. 'Look out of your own silly eyes when you wake up.' Puck takes off the ass's head.

85-6. For the Elizabethans dancing stood for harmony and marriage itself. Oberon and Titania *take hands* and dance to show they are re-united and their marriage healed, and together they *rock* the humans in a sleep from which they'll wake re-united and restored to their right minds.

87. *new in amity:* newly friends again. The springing beat and repeated rhyme of these lines (85-92) set the pace for the dance and help to create a sense of ceremonious joy.

88. *solemnly:* ceremoniously.

91-2- There will be a triple wedding.

93. *mark:* take notice.

94. *morning lark:* the lark sings to welcome the dawn. Puck, the fairy farthest from humanity, is anxious to stay with the night.

95. *sad:* sober.

96. *trip:* run lightly. *night's shade:* the darkness of night which retreats over the curve of the earth before the rising sun, but which the fairies with their supernatural speed can easily keep up with.

Dian's bud o'er Cupid's flower
Hath such force and blessed power.
Now, my Titania; wake you, my sweet queen.   75

Titania

My Oberon! What visions have I seen!
Methought I was enamour'd of an ass.

Oberon

There lies your love.

Titania   How came these things to pass?
O, how mine eyes do loathe his visage now!

Oberon

Silence awhile. Robin, take off this head.   80
Titania, music call; and strike more dead
Than common sleep of all these five the sense.

Titania

Music, ho, music, such as charmeth sleep!

Puck

Now when thou wak'st with thine own fool's eyes
    peep.

Oberon

Sound, music. Come, my Queen, take hands with me,   85

[*Music*]

And rock the ground whereon these sleepers be.
Now thou and I are new in amity,
And will to-morrow midnight solemnly
Dance in Duke Theseus' house triumphantly,
And bless it to all fair prosperity.   90
There shall the pairs of faithful lovers be
Wedded, with Theseus, all in jollity.

Puck

Fairy King, attend and mark;
I do hear the morning lark.

Oberon

Then, my Queen, in silence sad,   95
Trip we after night's shade.

97. *globe:* the round earth. *compass:* move round.

98. The fairies are as free and outside human laws as the *wand'ring moon.*

102. *on the ground:* Titania's love for Bottom brought her down to human level.

Stage Direction. Horns sound, the sun rises, and the city comes to the wood as Theseus and Hippolyta, dressed for hunting, enter among bustling attendants. The lovers, waking cured but puzzled, submit themselves to Theseus, who overrules Egeus and calls the couples home to Athens for an immediate triple wedding – for this is his own and Hippolyta's wedding day. *winding of horns:* blowing of hunting horns.

103. *forester:* game-keeper.

104. *observation:* ceremonial observance. Theseus and his court have got up early to keep the custom of welcoming Midsummer morning out of doors.

105. 'Since we have the early part of the day (*vaward=vanguard*) to spend . . .'

106. *music:* the cry of the hunting hounds.

107. *Uncouple:* 'unleash the hounds' (which were fastened together in pairs).

108. *Dispatch:* be quick.

110. *mark:* listen to. Hound voices echoing from the valley sides join in a combined din as satisfying as music to expert hunters like Theseus and the Amazon Hippolyta.

112. *Hercules and Cadmus:* ancient Greek mythological heroes.

113. *Crete:* a large island near Greece. *bay'd the bear:* forced the hunted bear to turn and face its pursuers.

114. *Sparta:* a Greek state. Both Crete and Sparta were famous for their fine hunting dogs.

115. *gallant chiding:* spirited barking. *besides:* as well as.

116. *every region near:* everywhere roundabout.

117. *Seem'd all one mutual cry.* The hounds' tremendous clamour, echoing from every side, seemed to come from everywhere at once.

117-18. 'I never heard clashing sounds that yet satisfied the ear so well, or such a delightful uproar.' Hippolyta found perfect enjoyment in a contradictory experience, a terrific din that delighted her like sweet music. Perhaps Shakespeare deliberately calls up the idea of such a complicated sensation at a moment when the contradictory forces of reason and blind desire in the lovers, and light and darkness in the world of the play, have at last struck a satisfying balance.

120. *So flew'd, so sanded:* with the same flews (loose hanging cheeks) and sandy colouring as Spartan hounds.

122. *Crook-knee'd:* bent-kneed, bandy. *dew-lapp'd:* with dewlaps (loose folds of skin hanging from the throat). *Thessalian bulls:* bulls bred in Thessaly, another part of Greece. Theseus' hounds seem to be like the Elizabethan Talbot, and the modern Basset hound.

We the globe can compass soon,
Swifter than the wand'ring moon.

Titania

Come, my lord; and in our flight,
Tell me how it came this night   *100*
That I sleeping here was found
With these mortals on the ground.

Exeunt
To the winding of horns, enter THESEUS, HIPPOLYTA,
EGEUS, *and* TRAIN

Theseus

Go, one of you, find out the forester;
For now our observation is perform'd,
And since we have the vaward of the day,   *105*
My love shall hear the music of my hounds.
Uncouple in the western valley; let them go.
Dispatch, I say, and find the forester.

Exit an ATTENDANT

We will, fair Queen, up to the mountain's top,
And mark the musical confusion   *110*
Of hounds and echo in conjunction.

Hippolyta

I was with Hercules and Cadmus once
When in a wood of Crete they bay'd the bear
With hounds of Sparta; never did I hear
Such gallant chiding, for, besides the groves,   *115*
The skies, the fountains, every region near,
Seem'd all one mutual cry. I never heard
So musical a discord, such sweet thunder.

Theseus

My hounds are bred out of the Spartan kind,
So flew'd, so sanded; and their heads are hung   *120*
With ears that sweep away the morning dew;
Crook-knee'd and dew-lapp'd like Thessalian bulls;

151

A MIDSUMMER NIGHT'S DREAM

123-4. ... with voices that harmonize like a ring of bells. There's some evidence that Elizabethan gentlemen liked to make up their hunting pack from a variety of hounds whose voices ranged from bass (deep-voiced) to treble (high and shrill).

124. *cry:* pack of hounds. *tuneable:* tuneful. Theseus, with his love of order, stresses the harmony of his pack's music.

125. *holla'd to:* cheered on with shouting. *cheer'd with horn:* encouraged with horn-calls.

127. *soft:* 'wait!' Theseus catches sight of the sleeping lovers just as the hunt is about to start. *nymphs:* lovely girls.

130. *old Nedar:* Helena's father.

132-3. *to observe The rite of May:* to celebrate Maytime, perhaps meaning 'summer'. But it looks as though Shakespeare has mixed up the May and Midsummer festivals here.

133. *intent:* purpose.

134. *in grace of our solemnity:* 'in honour of our celebration'.

136. It is Theseus' wedding-day when Hermia is to *answer her choice* between Demetrius and a convent (see Act I, Scene i, line 65).

138. *bid the huntsmen:* 'order the huntsmen to'. (The noise does not wake Bottom, sleeping heavily in the background.)

139. *Good-morrow:* good morning. The birds choose their mates on St. Valentine's day, February 14th. Theseus is teasing the lovers.

140. 'Are these woodland birds pairing only now?'

141. *Pardon:* 'forgive us'.

142. *rival enemies:* enemies competing for the same woman.

143. *How ... in the world ...?:* however? *concord:* peace.

144-5. 'That two men who hate each other are so unsuspicious (*free from jealousy*) that they're not afraid to sleep side by side.' Of course they fell asleep with hate in their hearts not knowing the other was there – but they wake healed and at peace.

146-53. Lysander, slowly shaking off the enchanted sleep, answers in a kind of trance. Though he can't really remember what's happened he is not afraid to face Theseus and wants to speak the truth. *amazedly:* in a state of bewilderment.

Slow in pursuit, but match'd in mouth like bells,
Each under each. A cry more tuneable
Was never holla'd to, nor cheer'd with horn,   *125*
In Crete, in Sparta, nor in Thessaly.
Judge when you hear. But, soft, what nymphs are
        these?

Egeus

My lord, this is my daughter here asleep,
And this Lysander, this Demetrius is,
This Helena, old Nedar's Helena.   *130*
I wonder of their being here together.

Theseus

No doubt they rose up early to observe
The rite of May; and, hearing our intent,
Came here in grace of our solemnity.
But speak, Egeus; is not this the day   *135*
That Hermia should give answer of her choice?

Egeus

It is, my lord.

Theseus

Go, bid the huntsmen wake them with their horns.

*Horns and shout within. The sleepers awake and
        kneel to* THESEUS

Good-morrow, friends. Saint Valentine is past;
Begin these wood-birds but to couple now?   *140*

Lysander

Pardon, my lord.

Theseus   I pray you all, stand up.
I know you two are rival enemies;
How comes this gentle concord in the world
That hatred is so far from jealousy
To sleep by hate, and fear no enmity?   *145*

Lysander

My lord, I shall reply amazedly,
Half sleep, half waking; but as yet, I swear,
I cannot truly say how I came here,

153

152-3. *where we might . . .* 'get married' Lysander means to say, but Egeus excitedly interrupts him. *peril of:* danger of being punished by.

154. *Enough:* Egeus thinks Lysander has said *enough* for Theseus (*you*) to condemn him.

157-9. *and me . . . be your wife.* Egeus, still caring nothing about his daughter's happiness, becomes hysterical at the threat to his authority. These are his last words in the play.

160-76. Demetrius also speaks the exact truth as he knows it, calmly and without ranting. At peace with themselves and each other, the lovers are independent yet respectful.

163. *in fancy:* for love.

164-5. Demetrius has escaped from isolation inside his own self-will; he knows now that his life can be swayed by something stronger than himself, though he doesn't know what it may be.

164. *I wot not:* 'I do not know'. What power has changed Demetrius?

167. *idle gaud:* worthless toy.

170. *object:* the centre of my attention.

172. *betroth'd:* engaged.

173-6. Love imagined in such down-to-earth ways has a chance of lasting. *like a sickness:* as in sickness, like someone who is ill. *this food:* Helena. Demetrius' infatuation for Hermia was like an illness which put him off Helena, his proper food.

174. *natural taste:* normal liking.

175. *it:* i.e., Helena.

177. '. . . it's lucky we've met you.'

178. *discourse:* story.

179. *overbear:* set aside. The lovers have settled their own affairs like adults, and Theseus confirms their decision. Old Egeus, behaving like a self-willed child, cannot be allowed to interfere.

181. *eternally be knit:* joined together for ever in marriage.

182. 'Since a good deal of the morning is now past.'

But, as I think—for truly would I speak,
And now I do bethink me, so it is—   *150*
I came with Hermia hither. Our intent
Was to be gone from Athens, where we might,
Without the peril of the Athenian law—

Egeus

Enough, enough, my Lord; you have enough;
I beg the law, the law upon his head.   *155*
They would have stol'n away, they would, Demetrius,
Thereby to have defeated you and me:
You of your wife, and me of my consent,
Of my consent that she should be your wife.

Demetrius

My lord, fair Helen told me of their stealth,   *160*
Of this their purpose hither to this wood;
And I in fury hither followed them,
Fair Helena in fancy following me.
But, my good lord, I wot not by what power—
But by some power it is—my love to Hermia,   *165*
Melted as the snow, seems to me now
As the remembrance of an idle gaud
Which in my childhood I did dote upon;
And all the faith, the virtue of my heart,
The object and the pleasure of mine eye,   *170*
Is only Helena. To her, my lord,
Was I betroth'd ere I saw Hermia.
But, like a sickness, did I loathe this food;
But, as in health, come to my natural taste,
Now I do wish it, love it, long for it,   *175*
And will for evermore be true to it.

Theseus

Fair lovers, you are fortunately met;
Of this discourse we more will hear anon.
Egeus, I will overbear your will;
For in the temple, by and by, with us   *180*
These couples shall eternally be knit.
And, for the morning now is something worn,

183. *purpos'd:* intended.

184. *three and three:* three men and three women, all three pairs.

187-98. The lovers, still half-asleep, can't sort out the waking and dreaming worlds. This uncomfortable double vision makes them unsure of themselves, full of wonder and less possessive in their love (lines 190-2). Perhaps they'll keep this new respect for other people and for things outside their own experience when they wake right up to ordinary life.

187. *These things:* everything that's happened. *undistinguishable:* hard to make out – just as it's hard to tell from a great distance whether shapes on the horizon are *mountains* or only *clouds* (line 188).

189. *Methinks:* 'it seems to me'. *parted eye:* eyes out of focus with each other. Hermia can't make out recent events; she feels as if she's seeing double.

190-2. Like something precious found by accident, Helena has found Demetrius without being sure he's really hers. She feels a kind of startled gratitude – and surely this is true love, to love someone who belongs to us without forgetting that we can't own them, that they belong to themselves as well.

195. *he did bid us:* he told us to.

197-9. Once the lovers know they are awake the night's experiences fall into place as 'dreams' which they can tell but which don't threaten to invade their waking life. *let's follow him.* Finally leaving the wood behind, the lovers set off for Athens and married life.

200-218. Bottom, like the lovers, is only half awake, and even more muddled than usual. He remembers the night like a dream of something greater than ordinary human experience. Indeed he repeats five times (204-13) that man can't understand this dream, and that he's a fool if he tries – although perhaps it can be made into a song.

200. Bottom thinks he's still at the rehearsal.

201. *Heigh-ho!* He yawns and opens his eyes.

203. *God's my life:* a surprised exclamation. *stol'n hence:* crept away.

204. *rare vision:* wonderful and extraordinary dream experience.

205. *wit:* mind.

206. *go about:* sets out. *expound:* explain.

Our purpos'd hunting shall be set aside.
Away with us to Athens, three and three;
We'll hold a feast in great solemnity.   *185*
Come, Hippolyta.

Exeunt THESEUS, HIPPOLYTA, EGEUS *and* TRAIN

Demetrius
    These things seem small and undistinguishable,
    Like far-off mountains turned into clouds.
Hermia
    Methinks I see these things with parted eye,
    When every thing seems double.
Helena   So methinks;   *190*
    And I have found Demetrius like a jewel,
    Mine own, and not mine own.
Demetrius   Are you sure
    That we are awake? It seems to me
    That yet we sleep, we dream. Do not you think
    The Duke was here, and bid us follow him?   *195*
Hermia
    Yea, and my father.
Helena   And Hippolyta.
Lysander
    And he did bid us follow to the temple.
Demetrius
    Why, then, we are awake; let's follow him;
    And by the way let us recount our dreams.

Exeunt

Bottom [*Awaking*]
    When my cue comes, call me, and I will answer. My   *200*
    next is 'Most fair Pyramus.' Heigh-ho! Peter Quince!
    Flute, the bellows-mender! Snout, the tinker!
    Starveling! God's my life, stol'n hence, and left me
    asleep! I have had a most rare vision. I have had a
    dream, past the wit of man to say what dream it was.   *205*
    Man is but an ass if he go about to expound this

157

209. *patch'd fool:* a fool dressed up in patchwork, the regular jester's costume.

210. . . . . I had. What Bottom had was an ass's head and the love of the fairy queen, too strange a mixture to be related to ordinary life.

210-13. Bottom, mixing the senses wildly, has the Bible (1 Corinthians, 2.9) at the back of his mind ('Eye hath not seen, nor ear heard, neither hath entered into the heart of man, the things which God hath prepared for them that love him.') Like Demetrius (lines 164-5) Bottom knows he has experienced something wonderful, bigger than himself and beyond human powers of understanding, something which can't be caught in a reasonable prose account but might inspire a song (line 213).

212. *conceive:* understand. *report:* tell.

214. *ballad:* song that tells a story. Though, since there's no reason in Bottom's dream, the song is unlikely to make much sense. Peter Quince has literary talents, as *Pyramus and Thisby* shows.

215. *hath no bottom:* there's no getting to the bottom of it.

216. *latter end:* concluding part. *a play.* Bottom is still hazy, but he knows he's acting in something.

217. *Peradventure:* perhaps. *gracious:* pleasing.

218. *her death:* Thisby's death, the most intense moment of the play they are to perform. Though there's no rational connection between Thisby's dying and *Bottom's Dream* they both mean a lot to Bottom.

SCENE II

The players' distress and disappointment – Bottom lost, the play spoilt – are the last of the night's bad effects to be put right. They are sitting miserably in Quince's house when Bottom rushes in and all is joyful excitement, as they look forward to the performance of *Pyramus and Thisby* that evening.

3. *transported:* transformed and carried off by the fairies.

4. *marr'd:* spoiled.

4-5. *it goes not forward:* 'it can't be put on'.

7. *discharge:* play.

8. *simply the best wit:* without exception the greatest talent.

8-9. *handicraft man:* manual worker.

dream. Methought I was—there is no man can tell
what. Methought I was, and methought I had, but
man is but a patch'd fool, if he will offer to say what
methought I had. The eye of man hath not heard, the *210*
ear of man hath not seen, man's hand is not able to
taste, his tongue to conceive, nor his heart to report,
what my dream was. I will get Peter Quince to write a
ballad of this dream. It shall be call'd 'Bottom's
Dream,' because it hath no bottom; and I will sing it *215*
in the latter end of a play, before the Duke.
Peradventure, to make it the more gracious, I shall
sing it at her death.

Exit

SCENE II—*Athens. Quince's house*

Enter QUINCE, FLUTE, SNOUT *and* STARVELING

Quince
Have you sent to Bottom's house? Is he come
home yet?
Starveling
He cannot be heard of. Out of doubt he is transported.
Flute
If he come not, then the play is marr'd; it goes not
forward, doth it?   5
Quince
It is not possible. You have not a man in all Athens
able to discharge Pyramus but he.
Flute
No; he hath simply the best wit of any handicraft
man in Athens.

10. *person:* appearance.

10-13. Quince means 'the very best' (*paragon*) but shocks Flute by saying *paramour* (sinful lover) an indecent word and a wicked thing (*thing of naught*) to his respectable mind.

16. *sport . . . forward:* 'if our play had gone on'.

16-17. *we had all . . . men:* 'we'd all have made our fortunes'.

18. Flute laments Bottom's loss.

19. *scaped:* escaped. Flute is convinced the Duke would have rewarded Bottom for his performance with a large pension for life.

20. *An:* if.

22-3. *in Pyramus:* as Pyramus.

24. Bottom charges in shouting and the whole mood changes. They jump to their feet and crowd round him. *hearts:* bold fellows.

25. *courageous.* Perhaps the word means 'brave' in the sense of 'splendid', but anyway Quince in his happy excitement says the first word that comes into his head.

27. *discourse:* tell. Only he doesn't tell and maybe never will.

32. *apparel:* costumes

Quince

Yea, and the best person too; and he is a very 10
paramour for a sweet voice.

Flute

You must say 'paragon.' A paramour is—God bless
us!—a thing of naught.

Enter SNUG

Snug

Masters, the Duke is coming from the temple; and
there is two or three lords and ladies more married. 15
If our sport had gone forward, we had all been made
men.

Flute

O sweet bully Bottom! Thus hath he lost sixpence a
day during his life; he could not have scaped
sixpence a day. An the Duke had not given him 20
sixpence a day for playing Pyramus, I'll be hanged.
He would have deserved it: sixpence a day in
Pyramus, or nothing.

Enter BOTTOM

Bottom

Where are these lads? Where are these hearts?

Quince

Bottom! O most courageous day! O most happy 25
hour!

Bottom

Masters, I am to discourse wonders; but ask me not
what; for if I tell you, I am not true Athenian. I will
tell you everything, right as it fell out.

Quince

Let us hear, sweet Bottom. 30

Bottom

Not a word of me. All that I will tell you is, that the
Duke hath dined. Get your apparel together; good

161

32-3. *good strings* – to tie their false beards on with.

33. *pumps:* light indoor slippers for dancing in.

34. *presently:* straightaway. *look o'er:* read through his part to make sure he knows it.

36. *preferr'd:* put on the short list from which Theseus will choose his evening's entertainment (Act V, Scene i, line 42). *clean linen:* clean underwear.

37. *pare:* cut.

39. *onions* and *garlic* make the breath smell.

40. *sweet breath:* sweet-smelling breath, and also delightful words.

41. *sweet comedy:* delightful comedy.

strings to your beards, new ribbons to your pumps;
meet presently at the palace; every man look o'er his
part; for the short and the long is, our play is   *35*
preferr'd. In any case, let Thisby have clean linen;
and let not him that plays the lion pare his nails, for
they shall hang out for the lion's claws. And, most
dear actors, eat no onions nor garlic, for we are to
utter sweet breath; and I do not doubt but to hear   *40*
them say it is a sweet comedy. No more words. Away,
go, away!

Exeunt

ACT FIVE

SCENE I

Act Five celebrates the royal wedding to which the whole play has looked forward from the start. The lovers are married, the actors happy to put on their play, and now all danger's past the hilarious and meaningless confusion of *Pyramus and Thisby* can be thoroughly enjoyed. Also, as Act I, Scene i was partly about love, so Act V, in which the play is performed, has ideas about dreaming and imagination running through it. Much of the act is pure comedy, but the end is hushed, when the lovers are in bed, the fire low, and the fairies come in to bless the house from the night outside.

1. 'The story these lovers tell is a strange one.'

2-22. Theseus' famous speech is a kind of companion to Bottom's (Act IV, Scene i, lines 200-18). Bottom rejected reason altogether and fell back on imagination to get his 'dream' across. Theseus rejects imagination, arguing simply that anything reason can't grasp is imaginary and can't be true. Neither's right – to be utterly without reason is to be less than human, an ass, as Bottom is – but perhaps in this case (as we know from watching the fairies and mortals in the wood) he's nearer the truth than the wise Theseus.

3. *antique fables:* weird old imaginary stories. *fairy toys:* ridiculous fairy-tales.

4-6. Lovers' and madmen's bubbling (*seething*) brains see more than reason can – and, Theseus implies, more than is really there.

5. *shaping fantasies:* inventive imaginations. *apprehend:* imagine.

6. *comprehends:* takes in.

7-8. 'Lunatics, lovers and poets are entirely made up of imagination.' Of course, all imagination and no reason does shut you up in yourself and cut you off from the world like a madman – or like the lovers in the wood.

10. *all as frantic:* just as raging mad.

11. *Helen's beauty:* perfect beauty. Helen of Troy was supposed to be the most beautiful woman who ever lived – the Elizabethans would imagine her as fair. *A brow of Egypt:* a dark gipsy face. Does Theseus' own love for Hippolyta boil down to nothing more than wishful thinking?

12-17. Theseus describes the poet's creative imagination, making something out of nothing. He criticizes poetry because he thinks it's pure day-dreaming, making up a nicer world than the one we've got (lines 18-20). But Shakespeare, through Theseus' mouth, seems to justify his own art, since *MND* itself does not turn its back on the world but means something – is, indeed, partly about this very problem of relating imagination to reason which Theseus shelves by dismissing imagination as make-believe.

12. *The poet's eye* here means the poet's imagination, his inner eye, which constantly searches the universe for fresh ideas. *fine frenzy:* splendid fever.

164

ACT FIVE

SCENE I—*Athens. The palace of Theseus*

Enter THESEUS, HIPPOLYTA, PHILOSTRATE, LORDS
and ATTENDANTS

Hippolyta
'Tis strange, my Theseus, that these lovers speak of.
Theseus
More strange than true. I never may believe
These antique fables, nor these fairy toys.
Lovers and madmen have such seething brains,
Such shaping fantasies, that apprehend   5
More than cool reason ever comprehends.
The lunatic, the lover, and the poet,
Are of imagination all compact.
One sees more devils than vast hell can hold;
That is the madman. The lover, all as frantic,   10
Sees Helen's beauty in a brow of Egypt.
The poet's eye, in a fine frenzy rolling,

13. 'Flashes back and forth through the entire universe.'

14-15. 'And as imagination gives birth to the images of strange new things . . .'

16. *shapes:* definite shapes. *airy nothing:* unreality (*airy*='thin as air' and so 'unreal').

17. *A local habitation:* a particular place to exist in.

19-20. 'If it only wants to feel (*apprehend*) some joy it thinks of (*comprehends*) something to bring it.' Imagination is a day-dreamer, able to create make-believe pleasures whenever it wants them.

21. *some fear:* something frightening.

22. *easy:* easily.

23-7. Hippolyta, unlike Theseus, is ready to admit there may be things beyond the reach of her reason, and so she doesn't close her mind to the evidence.

24. *transfigur'd:* changed.

25-6. 'Is proof of something more than mere imagination, and adds up to something certain' (*of great constancy*).

27. *howsoever:* in any case. *admirable:* to be wondered at.

30. *Accompany:* go along with as friends. *More:* i.e., more joy.

31. 'Attend you as a servant wherever you go, when you eat and when you sleep.'

32. *masques:* musical plays with elaborate scenery, costumes and dances, put on in noble houses to celebrate great occasions.

34. *after-supper:* dessert.

35. *manager of mirth:* entertainment organizer.

36. *in hand:* ready.

37. Waiting for bed-time is like torture for the lovers. Probably because he's mature and self-controlled, able to make physical desire obey his reason, it's Theseus who gives sex the biggest place in love (while the young lovers' intense passion is strangely disembodied).

39. *abridgment:* short play to make the time seem shorter.

40. *beguile:* while away. For Theseus plays and so on are no more than ways of killing time; they have no serious value. Shakespeare may be getting at the superior attitude of his own aristocratic audience here.

Doth glance from heaven to earth, from earth to
   heaven;
And as imagination bodies forth
The forms of things unknown, the poet's pen   *15*
Turns them to shapes, and gives to airy nothing
A local habitation and a name.
Such tricks hath strong imagination
That, if it would but apprehend some joy,
It comprehends some bringer of that joy;   *20*
How in the night, imagining some fear,
How easy is a bush suppos'd a bear?

Hippolyta
But all the story of the night told over,
And all their minds transfigur'd so together,
More witnesseth than fancy's images,   *25*
And grows to something of great constancy,
But howsoever strange and admirable.

    Enter LYSANDER, DEMETRIUS, HERMIA *and* HELENA

Theseus
Here come the lovers, full of joy and mirth.
Joy, gentle friends, joy and fresh days of love
Accompany your hearts!
Lysander   More than to us   *30*
Wait in your royal walks, your board, your bed!
Theseus
Come now; what masques, what dances shall we have,
To wear away this long age of three hours
Between our after-supper and bed-time?
Where is our usual manager of mirth?   *35*
What revels are in hand? Is there no play
To ease the anguish of a torturing hour?
Call Philostrate.
Philostrate   Here, mighty Theseus.
Theseus
Say, what abridgment have you for this evening?
What masque? what music? How shall we beguile   *40*

41. Time is *lazy* because it moves so slowly for the eager lovers.

42. *brief:* list. *ripe:* ready.

44. *Centaurs:* fabulous creatures, half-man and half-horse. According to legend, Theseus himself led the battle against them, but, as a hero should, he modestly gives the glory to his great relative, Hercules.

45. *eunuch:* a castrated man – he would probably have a high 'male soprano' voice.

47. *my kinsman:* Theseus and Hercules were cousins on the mother's side.

48-9. Wild women (*the tipsy Bacchanals*) tore Orpheus, the famous musician from Thrace (*the Thracian singer*) into little pieces when he stumbled on their secret celebration of the mysteries of Bacchus, god of wine. *riot:* frenzied orgy. *tipsy:* drunken.

50. *device:* show.

51. *last:* last time. *Thebes:* a Greek city, which Theseus conquered. (There was also an Egyptian Thebes.)

52. *The thrice three Muses:* the nine goddesses of learning and the arts.

53. *late deceas'd:* who died lately.

54-5. *satire:* a poem, story, play or sketch that indignantly mocks the failings of society. Theseus feels that a bitter (*keen*) complaint about the neglect of learning is unsuitable for (*Not sorting with*) a wedding.

56. *tedious:* boringly long – the opposite of *brief.*

57. *mirth:* joyful entertainment. The play's description contradicts itself – a happy tragedy is as impossible as *hot ice* (line 59).

59. *wondrous strange:* very odd. Some editors think Shakespeare must have written 'orange', not *strange;* otherwise there is not the same paradox as in *hot ice.*

60. 'How shall we harmonize this confusion?' The confusion in the lovers' lives has already been harmonized – now they can enjoy the purely comic disorder of *Pyramus and Thisby.*

65. *apt:* suited to its purpose. *fitted:* well-cast.

70. *passion:* violent feeling. The unintentionally funny tragedy made Philostrate laugh till he cried.

The lazy time, if not with some delight?
Philostrate
    There is a brief how many sports are ripe;
    Make choice of which your Highness will see first.

                    Giving a paper

Theseus
    'The battle with the Centaurs, to be sung
    By an Athenian eunuch to the harp.'   45
    We'll none of that: that have I told my love,
    In glory of my kinsman Hercules.
    'The riot of the tipsy Bacchanals,
    Tearing the Thracian singer in their rage.'
    That is an old device, and it was play'd   50
    When I from Thebes came last a conqueror.
    'The thrice three Muses mourning for the death
    Of Learning, late deceas'd in beggary.'
    That is some satire, keen and critical,
    Not sorting with a nuptial ceremony.   55
    'A tedious brief scene of young Pyramus
    And his love Thisby; very tragical mirth.'
    Merry and tragical! tedious and brief!
    That is hot ice and wondrous strange snow.
    How shall we find the concord of this discord?   60
Philostrate
    A play there is, my lord, some ten words long,
    Which is as brief as I have known a play;
    But by ten words, my lord, it is too long,
    Which makes it tedious; for in all the play
    There is not one word apt, one player fitted.   65
    And tragical, my noble lord, it is;
    For Pyramus therein doth kill himself.
    Which when I saw rehears'd, I must confess,
    Made mine eyes water; but more merry tears
    The passion of loud laughter never shed.   70
Theseus
    What are they that do play it?

72. *Hard-handed men:* manual workers.

73. *Which:* who.

74-5. *toil'd . . . nuptial:* 'worn out their untrained memories with learning this play for your wedding'.

79-80. *sport:* amusement. *intents:* (a) efforts, strained to the limit (*extremely stretch'd*); (b) the object of their efforts, their parts, painfully learned (*conn'd*) to please Theseus.

82. *amiss:* out of place.

83. *simpleness:* straightforwardness. *tender:* offer.

84. The play must be staged so that neither 'audience' nor 'players' have their backs to the real audience. If Theseus and his guests sit at the side the play can be acted half towards them and half towards the front of the house.

85. *wretchedness o'er-charged:* poor ignorant people trying to do what's beyond them. Hippolyta, who is sensitive and kind, doesn't want to see the actors make fools of themselves.

86. 'Service offered to a superior failing in the attempt to please.'

88-90. Theseus puns on *this kind* ('this kind of thing'=acting) and *kinder* ('more generous'), and again on *take* (both 'accept with good humour' and 'understand') and *mistake* ('get wrong').

91-105. Theseus is royal – he's had to learn to put up with boring public functions as part of his job. What he looks for isn't a high standard but the loving and loyal intention to please and honour him as ruler. Which makes him (though a shade inhuman) patient, polite, and able to find good in the clumsiest performance.

91-2. *noble respect . . . merit:* generous and well-bred consideration takes the doers' limited powers (*might*) into account and so doesn't condemn the low value (*merit*) of the deed.

93. *Where:* i.e., the places Theseus has visited on state progresses round his dukedom. (Queen Elizabeth I was famous for her progresses.) *clerks:* scholars. *purposed:* meant.

94. *premeditated welcomes:* prepared speeches of welcome.

96. *periods:* full-stops.

97-8. 'Choke off their fluent speech in their fright, and in the end break off speechless.'

Philostrate
    Hard-handed men that work in Athens here,
    Which never labour'd in their minds till now;
    And now have toil'd their unbreathed memories
    With this same play against your nuptial.   75
Theseus
    And we will hear it.
Philostrate   No, my noble lord,
    It is not for you. I have heard it over,
    And it is nothing, nothing in the world;
    Unless you can find sport in their intents,
    Extremely stretch'd and conn'd with cruel pain,   80
    To do you service.
Theseus   I will hear that play;
    For never anything can be amiss
    When simpleness and duty tender it.
    Go, bring them in; and take your places, ladies.

Exit PHILOSTRATE

Hippolyta
    I love not to see wretchedness o'er-charged,   85
    And duty in his service perishing.
Theseus
    Why, gentle sweet, you shall see no such thing.
Hippolyta
    He says they can do nothing in this kind.
Theseus
    The kinder we, to give them thanks for nothing.
    Our sport shall be to take what they mistake;   90
    And what poor duty cannot do, noble respect
    Takes it in might, not merit.
    Where I have come, great clerks have purposed
    To greet me with premeditated welcomes;
    Where I have seen them shiver and look pale,   95
    Make periods in the midst of sentences,
    Throttle their practis'd accent in their fears,
    And, in conclusion, dumbly have broke off,

99. *Trust me:* believe me.

100. *pick'd:* made out.

101. *the modesty of fearful duty:* the diffidence of awe-struck loyalty.

102. *rattling:* racing.

103. *saucy and audacious eloquence:* 'an impertinent chatterbox'.

105. 'In my opinion (*to my capacity*) say the most in fewest words.'

106. *address'd:* ready.

108-17. In reading this polite apology for the play Quince punctuates so badly that he says the exact opposite of what he means. Instead of explaining that the actors are here to please, he ends up saying they've come to annoy their audience!

108. *offend:* 'don't please you'.

109. *offend:* 'annoy you'.

110. *skill:* ability.

111. *beginning:* cause. *end:* purpose.

112. *but in despite:* only scornfully.

113. *minding to content you:* 'meaning to please you'.

114. *intent:* intention.

115. *repent you:* 'be sorry you've seen our play'.

116. *show:* mime. In Elizabethan plays the outline of the story was sometimes acted quickly without words before the proper performance began.

118. *stand upon points:* 'take care of his punctuation', and also, since Quince has been unintentionally rude, 'stand on ceremony'.

119. *rid:* 'ridden' and also 'got rid of'. *rough colt:* unbroken young horse.

120. *the stop:* both 'how to stop a horse' and 'where punctuation marks should come'.

120-1. *it is not enough to speak, but to speak true.* One of the things the lovers have learnt is that talking hard gets you nowhere if it makes no sense to other people. They've learnt to communicate, but the players, who have no sense, never will – they'll just go on acting tragically with comic effects, and speaking energetically without rational meaning.

120. *moral:* lesson.

121. *true:* accurately. (Notice the words *true, government* (123), *disordered* (125): truth, order and 'government' or control are highly valued in *MND*, and throughout Shakespeare's work.

123. *a recorder:* a simple wind instrument. *in government:* under control.

Not paying me a welcome. Trust me, sweet,
Out of this silence yet I pick'd a welcome;   *100*
And in the modesty of fearful duty
I read as much as from the rattling tongue
Of saucy and audacious eloquence.
Love, therefore, and tongue-tied simplicity
In least speak most to my capacity.   *105*

Re-enter PHILOSTRATE

Philostrate
So please your Grace, the Prologue is address'd.
Theseus
Let him approach.

Flourish of trumpets
Enter QUINCE *as the* PROLOGUE

Prologue
If we offend, it is with our good will.
That you should think, we come not to offend,
But with good will. To show our simple skill,   *110*
That is the true beginning of our end.
Consider then, we come but in despite.
We do not come, as minding to content you,
Our true intent is. All for your delight
We are not here. That you should here repent you,   *115*
The actors are at hand; and, by their show,
You shall know all, that you are like to know,
Theseus
This fellow doth not stand upon points.
Lysander
He hath rid his prologue like a rough colt; he knows
not the stop. A good moral, my lord: it is not enough *120*
to speak, but to speak true.
Hippolyta
Indeed he hath play'd on this prologue like a child on
a recorder—a sound, but not in government.

124-5. 'All the words were there (*nothing impaired*) but they didn't make sense (*all disordered*).'

125. *Who is next?* The idiocy of the mechanical play stirs up the audience to show off their own wit in sophisticated back-chat. Theseus joins in, but checks the fun when it threatens to interrupt the play and hurt the players' feelings (though once or twice it goes too far).

126-50. As *Prologue* (Quince) names them the players march on and act the story out. They may have trouble fitting the right actions to the right words. Their costumes are probably elaborate but unsuccessful: Thisby's mask (See Act I, Scene ii, line 45) and the skirts get in his way, Pyramus has an enormous brightly-coloured beard (Act I, Scene ii, lines 86-9) and a huge sword, and Wall is weighed down with *lime and rough cast* (line 130).

126. *Gentles:* 'Ladies and gentlemen'.

129. *certain:* without any doubt.

130. *lime and rough-cast:* building materials. *present:* stand for.

131. *sunder:* separate.

132. *poor souls:* poor things.

134. The *dog* may be a toy, as Moon has no trouble with it.

136. *think no scorn:* 'weren't too proud'.

138. *grisly:* horrifying. *hight:* is called (an out-of-date 'poetic' word).

140. *affright*, which means exactly the same as *scare*, is put in to fill out the line.

141. *mantle:* cloak. *did fall:* dropped.

143. *Anon:* at once. *tall:* brave.

144. *mantle slain:* the blood-stained cloak makes Pyramus think Thisby must be killed. You can't kill a cloak, but the play mixes up people and things, (e.g. Wall), as well as people and animals, (e.g. Lion), seeing and hearing, 190-1, and sense itself, 294-5.

145-6. Excessive jerky alliteration marks what should be the peak of tragic excitement, Pyramus' death.

blade: sword. *broached:* pierced (like tapping a barrel of beer). *boiling:* with passion.

147. 'Lingering in the shade of a mulberry tree': Thisby is out of sight among the bushes.

149. *twain:* two.

150. *at large:* at length (a promise they keep!).

151. *be to:* will.

Theseus

His speech was like a tangled chain; nothing impaired,
but all disordered. Who is next?   125

Enter, with a trumpet before them, as in dumb show,
PYRAMUS *and* THISBY, WALL, MOONSHINE *and* LION

Prologue

Gentles, perchance you wonder at this show;
But wonder on, till truth make all things plain.
This man is Pyramus, if you would know;
This beauteous lady Thisby is certain.
This man, with lime and rough-cast, doth present   130
Wall, that vile Wall which did these lovers sunder;
And through Wall's chink, poor souls, they are content
To whisper. At the which let no man wonder.
This man, with lanthorn, dog, and bush of thorn,
Presenteth Moonshine; for, if you will know,   135
By moonshine did these lovers think no scorn
To meet at Ninus' tomb, there, there to woo.
This grisly beast, which Lion hight by name,
The trusty Thisby, coming first by night,
Did scare away, or rather did affright;   140
And as she fled, her mantle she did fall;
Which Lion vile with bloody mouth did stain.
Anon comes Pyramus, sweet youth and tall,
And finds his trusty Thisby's mantle slain;
Whereat with blade, with bloody blameful blade,   145
He bravely broach'd his boiling bloody breast;
And Thisby, tarrying in mulberry shade,
His dagger drew, and died. For all the rest,
Let Lion, Moonshine, Wall, and lovers twain,
At large discourse while here they do remain.   150

Exeunt PROLOGUE, PYRAMUS, THISBY, LION
and MOONSHINE

Theseus

I wonder if the lion be to speak.

152. *No wonder:* 'it wouldn't be a miracle'.

153. *asses:* fools.

154. The play begins. Wall (and Lion, lines 215-22) explain themselves in verse that might as well be prose, but the emotional parts of Pyramus and Thisby make up for this. Quince uses stock poetic devices like the comparison with famous lovers (lines 195-8), and the piling-up of alliterative adjectives (line 264), but mostly feeling is built up by the simple method of saying the same word over and over again, along with passionate appeals to Night, Wall, Moon, the Furies, Fates, Nature, Lovers, and the Fates again. A great deal is said, very little happens, and there's no sense at all.

154. *interlude:* little play.

157. *crannied hole:* hole like a crack.

160. How would you make Wall's costume?

162. *this:* Wall holds out his hand with fingers parted. *right and sinister:* running right and left – a horizontal crack.

163. *fearful:* nervous. They are afraid their parents will catch them.

164. *lime and hair* are more of Wall's materials.

165. *wittiest:* cleverest. *partition:* both 'wall' and 'part of a speech'. *discourse:* speak.

168-71. The *night* of Pyramus and Thisby's tragedy is a comic echo of night (as the time of lovers' meeting, of fear, danger, and the threat of death) in *MND* itself.

168. *grim-look'd:* forbidding-looking. *hue:* colour.

169. 'O night, which always is when day isn't.'

175. *blink:* glance. *eyne:* eyes.

176. *courteous:* well-mannered.

Demetrius
No wonder, my lord: one lion may, when many
    asses do.

Wall
In this same interlude it doth befall
That I, one Snout by name, present a wall;   *155*
And such a wall as I would have you think
That had in it a crannied hole or chink,
Through which the lovers, Pyramus and Thisby,
Did whisper often very secretly.
This loam, this rough-cast, and this stone, doth show   *160*
That I am that same wall; the truth is so;
And this the cranny is, right and sinister,
Through which the fearful lovers are to whisper.

Theseus
Would you desire lime and hair to speak better?

Demetrius
It is the wittiest partition that ever I heard discourse, *165*
    my lord.

Enter PYRAMUS

Theseus
Pyramus draws near the wall; silence.

Pyramus
O grim-look'd night! O night with hue so black!
O night, which ever art when day is not!
O night, O night, alack, alack, alack,   *170*
I fear my Thisby's promise is forgot!
And thou, O wall, O sweet, O lovely wall,
That stand'st between her father's ground and mine;
Thou wall, O wall, O sweet and lovely wall,
Show me thy chink, to blink through with mine eyne. *175*

[WALL *holds up his fingers*]

Thanks, courteous wall. Jove shield thee well for this!
But what see I? No Thisby do I see.
O wicked wall, through whom I see no bliss;

180. *sensible:* alive.

182-5. Bottom takes Theseus quite seriously and can't resist joining in the conversation, even though it means stepping outside his part.
183. *spy:* catch sight of.
184. *fall pat:* happen just.
185. *yonder:* over there.

189. *knit up:* fastened together.

190-1. Bottom never fails to mix up seeing and hearing. *an:* if.

194. *lover's grace:* gracious lover.
195. *Limander:* Pyramus may mean Leander; if so his love should be Hero, not *Helen.* (Leander swam the Hellespont by night to visit Hero and was drowned.)
196. *the Fates:* the three goddesses who were supposed to spin and finally cut the thread of each man's life.
197. *Shafalus:* a mistake for Cephalus whose fidelity to his wife Procris (*Procrus*) was the subject of legend.

199. *vile:* worthless.

201. In spite of Quince's coaching, Bottom still says *Ninny* ('fool') instead of Ninus.

Curs'd be thy stones for thus deceiving me!
Theseus

The wall, methinks, being sensible, should curse 180
again.
Pyramus

No, in truth, sir, he should not. *Deceiving me* is
Thisby's cue. She is to enter now, and I am to spy her
through the wall. You shall see it will fall pat as I told
you; yonder she comes. 185

Enter THISBY

Thisby

O wall, full often hast thou heard my moans,
For parting my fair Pyramus and me!
My cherry lips have often kiss'd thy stones,
Thy stones with lime and hair knit up in thee.
Pyramus

I see a voice; now will I to the chink, 190
To spy an I can hear my Thisby's face.
Thisby!
Thisby

My love! thou art my love, I think.
Pyramus

Think what thou wilt, I am thy lover's grace;
And like Limander am I trusty still. 195
Thisby

And I like Helen, till the Fates me kill.
Pyramus

Not Shafalus to Procrus was so true.
Thisby

As Shafalus to Procrus, I to you.
Pyramus

O, kiss me through the hole of this vile wall.
Thisby

I kiss the wall's hole, not your lips at all. 200
Pyramus

Wilt thou at Ninny's tomb meet me straightway?

202. *Tide:* come.

203. *discharged:* played.

205. *used:* 'the Moon is the only go-between left.'

206. *No remedy:* 'it can't be helped'.
206-7. 'Walls with minds of their own, who may be listening when lovers least expect it (*without warning*) are better down.'

208. Hippolyta reacts simply to the play: she is embarrassed, uneasy, and bored.

209-10. 'The best plays are only weak copies of real life (*shadows*); and the worst are no worse than that, if imagination helps them out.' Because Theseus dismisses all plays as unreal and therefore not worth serious attention, he's tolerant and willing to use his imagination to sympathize with this one. Through the dreadful verse and worse acting he sees the players' pride and belief in themselves and their honest eagerness to please, and responds to that.
211. Theseus has imagination, though he doesn't think it's very important – the players themselves have none.
212-13. Theseus means that the actors think very well of themselves. *they may pass:* 'they'll count as'. He recognizes that they are impressed by their play if the audience are not.
214. *noble:* splendid. *beasts:* animals. In his lack of reason, Moon is likely to be as much an animal as Lion.
216. *monstrous:* 'horrible' but also 'enormous' – not the best description for a mouse. If the mouse is mighty, the lion's tame as a mouse, just as the wall's alive, the moon down-to-earth, and the men silly asses – all of them comic monsters in their way.
217. *quake:* shake with fear.
219-20. 'I am a terrible (*fell*) lion only in so far as I am Snug the joiner.' That is, not at all. Nor is he a lioness (*lion's dam*=lion's mother). There may also be a pun on *fell* meaning 'skin' – Snug is wearing a lion-skin costume.
221. *in strife:* as an enemy.
222. *'twere pity on my life:* 'I'd deserve hanging'.
223-52. The men tease Lion and Moon, though their complicated jokes and double meanings are far above the players' heads. Moon dislikes being interrupted and takes offence.
223. *gentle:* polite. *of a good conscience:* considerate.

Thisby
> *Tide life, tide death, I come without delay.*

Exeunt PYRAMUS *and* THISBY

Wall
> *Thus have I, Wall, my part discharged so;*
> *And, being done, thus Wall away doth go.*

Exit WALL

Theseus
> Now is the moon used between the two neighbours.   205

Demetrius
> No remedy, my lord, when walls are so wilful to hear
> without warning.

Hippolyta
> This is the silliest stuff that ever I heard.

Theseus
> The best in this kind are but shadows; and the worst
> are no worse, if imagination amend them.   210

Hippolyta
> It must be your imagination then, and not theirs.

Theseus
> If we imagine no worse of them than they of
> themselves, they may pass for excellent men. Here
> come two noble beasts in, a man and a lion.

Enter LION *and* MOONSHINE

Lion
> *You, ladies, you, whose gentle hearts do fear*   215
> *The smallest monstrous mouse that creeps on floor,*
> *May now, perchance, both quake and tremble here,*
> *When lion rough in wildest rage doth roar.*
> *Then know that I as Snug the joiner am*
> *A lion fell, nor else no lion's dam;*   220
> *For, if I should as lion come in strife*
> *Into this place, 'twere pity on my life.*

Theseus
> A very gentle beast, and of a good conscience.

224. *best* and *beast* probably sounded the same in Elizabethan pronunciation.

225-31. *Lion* traditionally stands for courage, *fox* for cunning, and *goose* for stupidity and cowardice.
225. 'As far as courage goes, he's a true fox' – more sly than brave.
226. 'And as far as sense (*discretion*) goes, a goose' – very silly.

227-8. Lion can't be fox-and-goose, 'because his courage is too weak for his caution' (another meaning of *discretion*).

229-30. 'I'm sure his sense isn't stronger than his courage.' Theseus means that Lion has no sense and no courage either.
230. *It is well:* 'That's enough'.
230-1. *Leave it to his discretion:* 'Let him decide how to behave'.

232-50. All Moonshine's props don't make a convincing moon and the audience pick holes in them till he gets fed-up and says his piece in prose, quite ruining any romantic atmosphere.
232. The word lantern (a lamp for outdoor use) could be spelled *Lanthorn.* Lanterns used to be made of horn.
233. Cuckolds (betrayed husbands) were supposed to have horns on their heads. Elizabethans never tired of this old joke.
234. *no crescent:* a round full moon. Perhaps Starveling (unlike most tailors and in defiance of his name) is fat.

237. *seem to be:* stand for.

238-40. If nothing's to be left to imagination, the realistic details must be accurate, and it's all wrong for the man to hold the moon (*the lantern*) in his hand. As man in the moon he should be inside it, which is impossible – just as it's impossible to get imaginative effects realistically (as Theseus and Shakespeare know, if Moon does not).

241. *for the candle:* for fear of being burnt.

242. *in snuff:* 'needing to be trimmed, to stop it smoking' and also, like Moon himself, 'in a temper'. Poor Moon is getting angry.

243. Hippolyta is bored by Moon and wishes he would go away.

244-5. This moon has little sense (*small light of discretion*) and so must be growing old (*in the wane*), as the shining arc of an old moon is small and gives little light.
245. *in courtesy:* for the sake of politeness.
246. *stay the time:* 'wait till Moon has finished his part'.

Demetrius
>The very best at a beast, my lord, that e'er I saw.

Lysander
>This lion is a very fox for his valour.   225

Theseus
>True; and a goose for his discretion.

Demetrius
>Not so, my lord; for his valour cannot carry his
>discretion, and the fox carries the goose.

Theseus
>His discretion, I am sure, cannot carry his valour;
>for the goose carries not the fox. It is well. Leave it to 230
>his discretion, and let us listen to the Moon.

Moon
>*This lanthorn doth the horned moon present—*

Demetrius
>He should have worn the horns on his head.

Theseus
>He is no crescent, and his horns are invisible within
>the circumference.   235

Moon
>*This lanthorn doth the horned moon present;*
>*Myself the Man i' th' Moon do seem to be.*

Theseus
>This is the greatest error of all the rest; the man
>should be put into the lantern. How is it else the man
>i' th' moon?   240

Demetrius
>He dares not come there for the candle; for, you see,
>it is already in snuff.

Hippolyta
>I am aweary of this moon. Would he would change!

Theseus
>It appears, by his small light of discretion, that he is
>in the wane; but yet, in courtesy, in all reason, we   245
>must stay the time.

248-50. Moon gives up trying to recite his speech and simply tells them the sense of it in prose.

257. Hippolyta is ashamed of her impatience and apologizes to Moon.

259. The lion has tossed and torn (*mous'd*) the cloak as a cat tears a mouse. But Theseus means to carry on the ridiculous contrast between Lion's fearsome looks and extraordinary gentleness.

262. *sunny:* the last word a poet would use to describe the moon.

Lysander
Proceed, Moon.
Moon
All that I have to say is to tell you that the lanthorn
is the moon; I, the Man i' the Moon; this thorn-bush,
my thorn-bush; and this dog, my dog.   250
Demetrius
Why, all these should be in the lantern; for all these
are in the moon. But silence; here comes Thisby.

Re-enter THISBY

Thisby
   This is old Ninny's tomb. Where is my love?
Lion [*Roaring*]
   O—

THISBY *runs off*

Demetrius
Well roar'd, Lion.   255
Theseus
Well run, Thisby.
Hippolyta
Well shone, Moon. Truly, the moon shines with a
good grace.

The LION *tears* THISBY'S *mantle, and exit*

Theseus
Well mous'd, Lion.

Re-enter PYRAMUS

Demetrius
And then came Pyramus.   260
Lysander
And so the lion vanish'd.
Pyramus
   Sweet Moon, I thank thee for thy sunny beams;
   I thank thee, Moon, for shining now so bright;
   For, by thy gracious, golden, glittering gleams,

264-5. 'I count on seeing Thisby by your light.'
266. Pyramus catches sight of the torn and blood-stained cloak.

268. *dole:* reason for sorrow.

274. *Furies:* cruel tormenting goddesses from hell.

276. *thread:* good threads. *thrum:* loose ends on the wrong side of a piece of cloth. So 'good and bad together, my whole life'. (Bottom, like the Fates themselves, is a weaver.)
277. *Quail:* destroy. *conclude:* make an end. *quell:* kill.
278-9. *passion:* agony, and the violent speech that expresses it. Theseus is not moved.

280. *Beshrew my heart:* 'bless me!' *but . . . man:* perhaps Hippolyta is saying 'I'm sorry for the man who could be upset by this!' – or possibly more simply sarcastic, 'I *am* sorry for poor Pyramus!'
281. *frame:* make.
282. *deflower'd:* raped (the wrong word – he means 'destroyed').

284. *cheer:* face.

285. *confound:* 'bring me to nothing'.

287. *pap:* breast.

289. *hop:* beat – a typically ridiculous choice of word.

290. *Thus . . . thus.* He stabs himself in four different places.
291. *Now am I dead.* He speaks too soon.

294-5. Even if *Tongue* and *Moon* changed places, this would scarcely make sense.

> *I trust to take of truest Thisby sight.*   265
>   *But stay, O spite!*
>   *But mark, poor knight,*
> *What dreadful dole is here!*
>   *Eyes, do you see?*
>   *How can it be?*   270
> *O dainty duck! O dear!*
>   *Thy mantle good,*
>   *What! stain'd with blood?*
> *Approach, ye Furies fell.*
>   *O Fates! come, come;*   275
>   *Cut thread and thrum;*
> *Quail, crush, conclude, and quell.*

Theseus
  This passion, and the death of a dear friend, would go
  near to make a man look sad.

Hippolyta
  Beshrew my heart, but I pity the man.   280

Pyramus
> *O wherefore, Nature, didst thou lions frame?*
> *Since lion vile hath here deflower'd my dear;*
> *Which is—no, no—which was the fairest dame*
> *That liv'd, that lov'd, that lik'd, that look'd with cheer.*
>   *Come, tears, confound;*   285
>   *Out, sword, and wound*
> *The pap of Pyramus;*
>   *Ay, that left pap,*
>   *Where heart doth hop.*

      [*Stabs himself*]

> *Thus die I, thus, thus, thus.*   290
>   *Now am I dead,*
>   *Now am I fled;*
> *My soul is in the sky.*
>   *Tongue, lose thy light;*
>   *Moon, take thy flight.*   295

297. *die:* one of a pair of dice. *ace:* (pronounced very like 'ass') the single spot marking 'one' on a *die.*

298. *nothing:* zero.

299. *surgeon:* doctor.

300. *prove:* turn out to be. *ass:* pun on ace (reminding us of Bottom's adventure, which Theseus knows nothing about).

304. *passion:* passionate speech.

307-9. Neither Pyramus nor Thisby is any good. *mote:* speck of dust. *balance:* scales. *warrant:* guard.

311. *videlicet:* 'in these words, namely' (an exact legal term not at all suited to poetry).

[*Exit* MOONSHINE]

Now die, die, die, die, die.

[*Dies*]

Demetrius
No die, but an ace, for him; for he is but one.
Lysander
Less than an ace, man; for he is dead; he is nothing.
Theseus
With the help of a surgeon he might yet recover and
prove an ass. 300
Hippolyta
How chance Moonshine is gone before Thisby comes
back and finds her lover?

Re-enter THISBY

Theseus
She will find him by starlight. Here she comes; and
her passion ends the play.
Hippolyta
Methinks she should not use a long one for such a 305
Pyramus; I hope she will be brief.
Demetrius
A mote will turn the balance, which Pyramus, which
Thisby, is the better—he for a man, God warrant us:
she for a woman, God bless us!
Lysander
She hath spied him already with those sweet eyes. 310
Demetrius
And thus she moans, videlicet:—
Thisby

> *Asleep, my love?*
> *What, dead, my dove?*
> *O Pyramus, arise,*
> > *Speak, speak. Quite dumb?* 315
> > *Dead, dead? A tomb*

324. *Sisters Three:* the Fates again.

326. Rather a beautiful line, and Thisby might for once speak it quietly and effectively.
327. *gore:* thick blood.
328. *shore:* cut through.
329. *shears:* scissors. *thread of silk:* the silk thread of his life.

332. *imbrue:* soak with blood – she stabs herself with Pyramus' sword. *Bottom [starting up]:* As if to underline once and for all that death doesn't happen in comedy, Bottom 'rises' from the dead – being unable, as usual, to keep out of the conversation.

338-9. *the wall is down that parted their fathers:* 'the separation between their families is over', as in *Romeo and Juliet*, when the families make friends too late, after the lovers are dead. *Pyramus and Thisby* is basically the same story as *Romeo and Juliet* (which shows the difference treatment can make), and *MND* itself, in which a father forbids two lovers to marry, could have had the same tragic ending.
339-40. Bottom mixes *see* and *hear* again. *Epilogue:* short speech at the end of the play, in Elizabethan drama usually apologizing for its faults and encouraging the audience to clap, like Puck's final words (lines 409-24).
340. *Bergomask:* a vigorous Italian country dance, probably in this case miming a wedding.
343. *excuse:* apology.
344-7. The end of *MND* would be quite spoilt if the workmen saw their play wasn't a success. Perhaps Theseus makes the joke that betrays his true opinion half to himself, before thanking them warmly and heartily.
344. *Marry:* truly.

> *Must cover thy sweet eyes.*
> *These lily lips,*
> *This cherry nose,*
> *These yellow cowslip cheeks,*   320
> *Are gone, are gone;*
> *Lovers, make moan;*
> *His eyes were green as leeks.*
> *O Sisters Three,*
> *Come, come to me,*   325
> *With hands as pale as milk;*
> *Lay them in gore,*
> *Since you have shore*
> *With shears his thread of silk.*
> *Tongue, not a word.*   330
> *Come, trusty sword;*
> *Come, blade, my breast imbrue.*

[*Stabs herself*]

> *And farewell, friends;*
> *Thus Thisby ends;*
> *Adieu, adieu, adieu.*   335

[*Dies*]

Theseus
Moonshine and Lion are left to bury the dead.
Demetrius
Ay, and Wall too.
Bottom [*Starting up*]
No, I assure you; the wall is down that parted their
fathers. Will it please you to see the Epilogue, or to
hear a Bergomask dance between two of our   340
company?
Theseus
No epilogue, I pray you; for your play needs no
excuse. Never excuse; for when the players are all
dead there need none to be blamed. Marry, if he that

345. *writ:* wrote.

346. *garter:* ribbon tied round the leg to hold up a stocking.

347. *notably discharg'd:* well performed.

348. *let . . . alone:* 'we won't have an epilogue'.
The dance could be danced by the whole company, lovers and all (though the aristocrats would probably not mix with the workmen). The pounding rhythms and vigorous high jumps and kicks would be infectiously gay and set the audience wanting to dance too.

349. *iron tongue:* clapper of the bell that strikes midnight. *told:* counted (with a pun on 'tolled' meaning 'rung').

350. *fairy time:* from midnight till dawn, when fairies are about. Theseus is joking: he doesn't believe in fairies. But the quiet of night is the time for love's magic, to which the lovers have eagerly looked forward all evening, and to which the whole play is only a preliminary.

351-2. 'Tomorrow we shall oversleep for as long as we've sat up late tonight.'

353. *palpable-gross:* plainly clumsy. *beguil'd:* 'taken our minds off'.

354. *heavy gait:* slow steps.

355. *solemnity:* celebration.

Stage Direction. Puck carries a brush to sweep away dust and with it everything evil. He purifies the house ready for the fairies to bless it, and his words are a spell of protection against the night outside.

357. *Now:* (repeated at the beginning of every four lines of Puck's spell) marks the time for love and enchantment, which has actually come at last.

357-68. Puck conjures up all night's dangers – wild beasts, misery, death and ghosts – before he shuts them out.

358. *behowls:* howls at.

359. *heavy:* tired.

360. *all . . . foredone:* quite worn out.

361. *wasted brands:* burnt-out logs.

362. *screech-owl:* the Barn Owl, whose harsh cry is supposed to be a warning of death.

363-4. 'Reminds poor unhappy people of death.'

364. *shroud:* the winding-sheet in which a corpse is wrapped for burial.

365-8. It is after midnight.

366. *gaping wide:* cracking wide open like black mouths.

367. *his sprite:* the ghost of whoever's buried there.

368. *church-way paths:* paths leading through the churchyard to the church. *glide:* flit silently along.

370. *Hecate:* an aspect of the three-fold (*triple*) moon goddess specially connected with witches and magic. The same goddess was called Cynthia (in heaven), Diana (on earth) and Proserpina – or, here, Hecate (in the underworld). *team:* the horses, one black, one white, that draw the moon across the sky.

371-2. For the last time, night is set against day. Though the dark is dangerous for humans it has the appeal of dreams – and it's the fairies' home.

writ it had played Pyramus, and hang'd himself in 345
Thisby's garter, it would have been a fine tragedy.
And so it is, truly; and very notably discharg'd. But
come, your Bergomask; let your epilogue alone.

A dance

The iron tongue of midnight hath told twelve.
Lovers, to bed; 'tis almost fairy time.   350
I fear we shall out-sleep the coming morn,
As much as we this night have overwatch'd.
This palpable-gross play hath well beguil'd
The heavy gait of night. Sweet friends, to bed.
A fortnight hold we this solemnity,   355
In nightly revels and new jollity.

Exeunt
Enter PUCK *with a broom*

Puck

Now the hungry lion roars,
And the wolf behowls the moon;
Whilst the heavy ploughman snores,
All with weary task fordone.   360
Now the wasted brands do glow,
Whilst the screech-owl, screeching loud,
Puts the wretch that lies in woe
In remembrance of a shroud.
Now it is the time of night   365
That the graves, all gaping wide,
Every one lets forth his sprite,
In the church-way paths to glide.
And we fairies, that do run
By the triple Hecate's team   370
From the presence of the sun,
Following darkness like a dream,

373. *frolic:* merry, playful.

374. *hallowed:* blessed. *house:* for human beings the house means home and safety.

375. *broom:* brush. *before:* i.e., before the other fairies.

376. As he speaks, Puck sweeps away the dust trapped in the corner behind the open door.

377. *glimmering:* faintly shining. The fairies carry soft lights.

378. *drowsy:* dull, low.

380. *brier:* bramble twig.

381. *ditty:* song.

382. *trippingly:* lightly and quickly.

383. 'Say over your song by heart.'

384. *warbling:* sweet and trilling.

Stage Direction. The song probably begins with Oberon's words *Now, until the break of day,* but perhaps the others do not join in until the third line. It seems to end with *Shall upon their children be.*

388. *stray:* wander about.

389. Oberon and Titania will bless Theseus and Hippolyta themselves. At Elizabethan marriages the priest blessed the bed with the couple in it.

391. *issue there create:* children conceived there.

393. *So:* in the same way.

395-6. 'Their children won't have any nasty birthmarks.'

397. *hare-lip:* divided upper lip, like the cleft lip of a hare.

398. *mark prodigious:* unlucky birthmark.

399. *nativity:* birth.

401. *consecrate:* blessed (fairy holy-water).

402. *take his gait:* make his way.

194

Now are frolic. Not a mouse
Shall disturb this hallowed house.
I am sent with broom before,   375
To sweep the dust behind the door.

Enter OBERON *and* TITANIA, *with all their* TRAIN

Oberon

Through the house give glimmering light,
By the dead and drowsy fire;
Every elf and fairy sprite
Hop as light as bird from brier;   380
And this ditty, after me,
Sing and dance it trippingly.

Titania

First, rehearse your song by rote,
To each word a warbling note;
Hand in hand, with fairy grace,   385
Will we sing, and bless this place.

OBERON *leading*, *the* FAIRIES *sing and dance*

Oberon

Now, until the break of day,
Through this house each fairy stray.
To the best bride-bed will we,
Which by us shall blessed be;   390
And the issue there create
Ever shall be fortunate.
So shall all the couples three
Ever true in loving be;
And the blots of Nature's hand   395
Shall not in their issue stand;
Never mole, hare-lip, nor scar,
Nor mark prodigious, such as are
Despised in nativity,
Shall upon their children be.   400
With this field-dew consecrate,
Every fairy take his gait,

403. *several chamber:* separate room.

407. 'Dance away and don't stop.'

Stage Direction. As the stage empties, Puck comes forward to make a polite apology for the play and ask the audience to clap.

409. *shadows:* all the actors, not just the fairies alone.

411. *slumber'd:* slept. This is disconcerting – if we can't tell the difference between watching a play and dreaming, how can we tell whether we're ever really awake, or whether perhaps all life is just a dream?

413-15. 'Ladies and gentlemen, don't find fault with (*reprehend*) this weak and unimportant story (*idle theme*), that only gives birth to a dream.' This, too, is less reassuring than it sounds, since we know from the play that 'dreams' can have serious meanings. But though there are these under-meanings, it is a comedy, and Puck's farewell is very lightly said.

416. 'We'll improve if you forgive us.'

418. *unearned:* undeserved.

419. *scape the serpent's tongue:* 'escape being hissed' (as a sign that the audience dislike the play).

420. 'We'll soon make up for it' – by acting better in a better play.

423. *give me your hands:* clap.

424. *restore amends:* 'make up for it all' – perhaps by bringing good luck to everyone. His mischievous side is well under control at the end.

And each several chamber bless,
Through this palace, with sweet peace;
And the owner of it blest   *405*
Ever shall in safety rest.
Trip away; make no stay;
Meet me all by break of day.

Exeunt all but PUCK

Puck

If we shadows have offended,
Think but this, and all is mended,   *410*
That you have but slumber'd here
While these visions did appear.
And this weak and idle theme,
No more yielding but a dream,
Gentles, do not reprehend.   *415*
If you pardon, we will mend.
And, as I am an honest Puck,
If we have unearned luck
Now to scape the serpent's tongue,
We will make amends ere long;   *420*
Else the Puck a liar call.
So, good night unto you all.
Give me your hands, if we be friends,
And Robin shall restore amends.

Exit

SUMMING UP

Love dominates *A Midsummer Night's Dream*, but it's much more than a love story. Among other things, it's a play that tells us what love and marriage are like, shot through with strong sexual emotion. If sex in real life is powerful, confusing and disturbing, it's not surprising that in the world of the play violence and discord break out. Desire acts like a drug. Under its influence the lovers hate as ecstatically as they love, and exciting extremes take the place of ordinary dull life.

> *I'll follow thee, and make a heaven of hell,*
> *To die upon the hand I love so well.*
>
> (Act II, Scene i, lines 243-4)

Love is free. No one can tell someone else who to love. So when Egeus orders his daughter to marry Demetrius she refuses and runs away with Lysander.

So in Act I, Scene i, love causes a family quarrel, and clashes head-on with a father's authority and the Law of Athens that backs that authority up. In fact the real quarrel is between Athenian society which approves of arranged marriages, social contracts into which the parties' own wishes don't enter at all, and gives parents absolute power over their children, and the teenage children's individual desires. The children know that only they can settle whom they love.

Athens makes romantic love impossible, and so the lovers run off to the dark wood watched only by the indifferent moon. As a result of their adventures there they discover whom they really love and sort themselves out into faithful couples ready for marriage. Then Athens accepts them back. Egeus' continued opposition is clearly bullying, wilful and unjust, and Theseus overrules him. It looks as though in a fight between society and romantic love romance has won.

Certainly Shakespeare is on the lovers' side. But if youth and love are right, and age and authority wrong, that's not the whole story. For if the outside world can't see that private feelings are real and must be respected, then when love acts on feeling alone and disregards the world it also loses touch with reality. Already in Act I Demetrius's unkindness has taught Helena this, and it's borne out by the experience of all the lovers in the wood.

Love is selfish. Far from uniting the lovers, desire separates them, for it makes them indifferent to each other as people. Each man chases the girl he wants as an object, a possession. 'Love' in fact is a violent impersonal force, that irons the humanity out of people, reducing them to animals, monsters, even things. At the climax of the final quarrel the four lovers see each other all crooked. Helena is a *painted maypole*, her height, slimness and bright colouring oddly exaggerated. Hermia is a *puppet* and a *dwarf*.

Why does love, which is tender and full of feeling, have such an effect on people? Helena describes love at the beginning of the play:

> *Things base and vile, holding no quantity,*
> *Love can transpose to form and dignity.*
>> (Act I, Scene i, lines 232-3)

Being in love is something like being drunk or drugged, when quite ordinary things temporarily swell into tremendous beauty and significance. Love flames up inside the lover and transforms his surroundings, specially the love-object herself. The girl may really be neither very beautiful nor worthwhile – never mind, the lover sees her as lovely and desirable even in spite of what his eyes and reason may be trying to tell him.

In this, love is like imagination – in *MND* the two sometimes seem to be almost the same thing. 'Fancy' can mean both love (*Fair Helena in fancy following me*), and something imagined or made up:

> *But all the story of the night told over . . .*
> *More witnesseth than fancy's images.*
>> (Act V, Scene i, lines 23-5)

And 'fantasy' brings the two even closer together; it means 'sexual imagination' like Titania's 'hateful fantasies'.

Over and over again love's 'insideness', its lack of connection with fact and what's going on in the outside world, is brought home. For Helena the dark night is light and the lonely wood full of company when Demetrius is there: *For you, in my respect, are all the world.* And because he doesn't love her, she loses all confidence in her own attractiveness – she thinks her ugliness scares the wild animals away, and that her mirror lied when it showed her to herself as lovely.

People in love, then, don't know what things are really like, they only know how they feel – and they feel very strongly indeed. Because love is so subjective and powerful it drives them – and especially the men – to pursue their changing desires more and more wildly and blindly. In the end their relations with each other break down altogether and their own identities begin to crack up. The Lysander who curses Hermia and the Lysander who adores her are like two different people, and neither he nor she can understand the change. She asks him:

> *Am I not Hermia? Are not you Lysander?*
> (Act III, Scene ii, line 273).

The breakdown comes in the long quarrel scene (III ii) when all four are on stage together for the first time. But it's the natural outcome of what their love has been like from the beginning, utterly self-willed and unaware of any feelings beside its own. Demetrius, for instance, eagerly joins in bullying Hermia to marry him against her will, not caring how she feels as long as he gets his own way. They are at complete cross-purposes:

> *The more I hate, the more he follows me,*

while Helena's love doesn't touch him at all:

> *The more I love, the more he hateth me.*
> (Act I, Scene i, lines 198-9)

Such love is not reasonable. And even the lovers expect love to make sense. Feeling itself isn't an argument for changing in love, there has to be a reason. And so when first Lysander and then Demetrius stop loving Hermia and for no reason start loving Helena (none of the lovers know about the magic juice) they simply are not believed.

In the end, words mean nothing. Each lover speaks from a full heart, but as everyone ignores what the others actually say and only answers what they think that they mean, total misunderstanding is the result. Helena answer Demetrius's true passion with *O spite! O hell!;* Hermia' 'sweet love' clashes with Lysander's *tawny Tartar.*

And when language becomes meaningless and com munication breaks down altogether the lovers find them selves in a crazy world. They are isolated, bewildered and desperately frustrated. This is why they begin to fight; since no one can hear them the only way left to make contact is by violence, and for the men at least this could easily end in the final silence of death. They finish cut off from each other and lost in the pitch dark, longing for morning when they can at least see to get out of the wood. This total loss of touch with anything or anybody outside themselves, which is what the loss of meaning in words, the inability to get through, stands for, is where absolute surrender to their intense personal feelings has led them. Love which was all the world, and which turned night to day, leaves them alone in the dark.

Of course it's the love-juice that has landed them in this desperate mess. But the juice (pure Cupid essence) only exaggerates the normal effects of love. Already in coming to the wood the lovers, trying to be free, have abandoned the day-lit, rational and moral world of civilized humanity. And Titania is in the same situation. Oberon punishes her with the juice because it can make her act out what she already is, since in throwing off her husband she has thrown off authority and reason and given herself up to her own disordered sensuality.

Her dealings with Bottom comically illustrate the difference between love's self-deception (*What angel wakes me from my flow'ry bed?*) and what the beloved is like in fact. 'Reason and love,' says Bottom 'keep little company nowadays.' People need both reason and emotion to be whole, and Titania has lost reason. When she embraces Bottom, her delicate beauty twining round his hairy ugli- ness makes a picture of what happens when reason and the senses, soul and body, get divided. He is an ass and she calls him an angel; she looks like an angel and is an ass; but they are still two contradictory parts that can never make up a whole.

The extremes in which the lovers see each other are evidence of the same split. If they don't see perfection (*O Helen, goddess, nymph, perfect, divine!*) then it's a hideous animal they see (*cat . . . vile thing . . . serpent*). Glowing word-pictures of love and friendship (*We, Hermia, like two artificial gods . . .*) break down into realistic abuse (*She was a vixen when she went to school*). Since neither gods nor animals are people, neither description is true.

In Act I, love, though ill-fated, dangerous and irrational, is also very beautiful. As soon as they reach the wood, the lovers start seeing themselves and each other as animals: spaniels, deer, tigers, bears, doves, ravens, vixens, cats, and (especially and repeatedly) as treacherous and deceitful snakes. Titania too wraps herself up in snakeskin, and Oberon spitefully wishes her the worst of animal lovers, monkey, ape or *boar with bristled hair*.

Quince's company of actors are as senseless as the lovers, and they are compared with animals as well. Puck likens Bottom's frightened friends to birds, and the lion is their own invention. In them reason and impulse are separated not because their emotions are strong but because their poor heads are weak. Fright robs Bottom's companions of whatever brains they have: and Bottom himself, who never had any, is fitted out with an ass-head as a sign that he's naturally donkey from the neck up. They are all fools, and Shakespeare presents them not even as pure beasts, but as comic monsters, the funny mixtures men become when reason's not on top. Snug's face appears through the lion's neck, Snout becomes a living Wall, and Starveling the man in the moon, to match Bottom's transformation into a monstrous ass.

For the actors in their folly are like lovers, shut away in their own world, untouched by reason, fact or outside opinion. They don't understand other people or get through to them either. If this weren't funny it would be sad, because acting and love are both above all ways of getting through, of sharing, and of saying things so that they can be understood.

The workmen-actors see themselves as noble and romantic, and they think their play is moving (*let the audience look to their eyes*) and frightening too: 'I fear it, I promise you' is Starveling's reaction to the Lion. But *we* see them very differently. Theseus, his guests, and the audience of *MND* all think they're funny.

This is true too of the lovers. To Puck and us their quarrel scene is like a play, with all the tricks of situation comedy, misunderstanding, exaggeration, stock characterization. The more earnestly the lovers take it, the funnier they get, till the scene dissolves into slapstick.

Clearly, the love tangle can be seen in two different ways. It's serious for the lovers but for the watchers it's farce. The audience laughs, but can't (unlike the non-human Puck) ignore the lovers' desperation. To lose touch with each other and with the world and be imprisoned in violent fantasies is one of the worst things that can happen to men, and it happens to the lovers.

The way *Pyramus and Thisby* parodies *MND* itself makes it still easier to look at the troubles of lovers in two ways at once. Pyramus and Thisby's situation is the same as Lysander's and Hermia's at the beginning of *MND*: they are two faithful lovers separated by cruel parents. Yet they are ridiculous – nothing funnier or less moving could be imagined, and it's only the tender-hearted Hippolyta who feels ashamed at not being able to take them seriously. Their solemnity parodies the lovers' earnestness, and Quince's poetry takes some of the shine out of the lovers' passionate and lofty style.

Yet *Pyramus and Thisby* is a tragedy, the tragedy that *MND* is not, but *Romeo and Juliet*, with exactly the same basic situation, is. It all depends on how the story is presented, and *Romeo and Juliet* achieves the high feeling and sad end that *Pyramus and Thisby* tries for and misses. By bringing death for love into the open, the story of Quince's play gives us a chance to see possible tragedy hidden in *MND* itself. The fact of death is never forgotten in *MND*, from Lysander's highly-strung and somehow challenging lament: *So quick bright things come to confusion* to Puck's relish for damned ghosts, wormy beds, and *graves all gaping wide*. The fear that love will be destroyed in the dark keeps coming back, as Hermia cries: *either death or you I'll find immediately* and accuses Demetrius of murdering Lysander; or Helena exclaims:

'tis partly mine own fault
Which death or absence soon shall remedy.
(Act III, Scene ii, lines 243-4)

And it is a real danger. Egeus wanted to have his daughter killed, and the men came near actually to killing each other.

Love is so intense and makes the lovers feel so alive that it reminds them of death, while the loss of love is like death and the beloved's cruelty 'kills' the lover. And it stirs up extreme and reckless feelings that make the lovers do wild and reckless things, as well as rousing determined, even deadly, opposition from the establishment.

Pyramus and Thisby, where fate is against the lovers, brings all this out into the open. At the same time by overplaying death and making it ridiculous, it drives out fear. Bottom as Pyramus kills tragedy dead. Indeed in the rehearsal scene the producer and cast plan elaborate precautions against their play's causing anyone – especially 'the ladies' – the slightest alarm or distress. . . . *let the prologue seem to say . . . that Pyramus is not kill'd indeed.* In their anxiety in case death by sword and lion should be taken 'for real', they successfully destroy any tragic illusion, anything that could touch you or make you forget for a moment that the play is not pretence. They leave only high comedy: *His eyes were green as leeks.* In this performance itself the comic pattern of life rising out of and overcoming death is acted out when Bottom springs up from his stage 'death' to join in the conversation. It's a moment of comic confusion (like the general confusion between tragedy and comedy, *very tragical mirth*). But it also parodies what happens in *MND* itself when the lovers rise from a sleep like death to a new and happy life. And this in turn relates to the central purpose of *MND*, to celebrate the defeat of death and barrenness by fertile marriage, from which lasting happiness and children spring.

Though death and the Lion are too convincing for the players, they want a realistic moon. To suggest moonlight in the verse is not enough, though Pyramus does that too (*O moon, I thank thee for thy sunny beams* . . .). They need a real moon as part of the scenery, and end up inventing Moonshine, with all his paraphernalia of thornbush, dog

205

and lantern – a most unromantic figure who's finally forced by his audience's laughter to speak his piece in prose.

Shakespeare really uses Moon to make a general point about how plays should be written and staged. The most detailed and realistic scenery can't ever be good enough to make you think you're looking at the real thing; indeed the more elaborate it is the likelier it is to draw attention to its own artificiality (*The man should be put into the lantern. How is it else the man i' th' moon?*). It's a point that needs remembering when staging *MND* itself – how can you have fairies small enough to fit in an acorn-cup? Shakespeare does it for us in the language of the play: scenery and effects, though useful (specially lighting) in creating atmosphere, will fail if they try to be realistic.

In *MND*, the moon is there, Phoebe, who

> *doth behold*
> *Her silver visage in the wat'ry glass,*
> *Decking with liquid pearl the bladed grass*
> (Act I, Scene i, lines 209-11)

Shakespeare's language gets through; it can move us, enchant us, thrill us or make us laugh, just as he wishes, when Bottom and the rest don't even get as far as talking sense. Indeed *MND* is a play where the language as sheer poetry rather than exchange between characters is specially important. Its high spots are all set-pieces which print some landscape with its proper atmosphere – spring's freshness, or the half-thrilling horror of the night – on our imagination.

Shakespeare uses the clumsy stage properties and ineffective verse of Quince's play to throw his own powers into strong relief. He can afford the doggerel of *Pyramus and Thisby*; he can even afford to draw attention to the staginess of his own heroes and heroines, because when he wants to convince us then he can. He makes fun of amateur acting and seems to side with his noble audience in despising plays, yet *MND* is a living demonstration that drama does communicate. *Pyramus and Thisby* is funny because it's a caricature of the real thing. So also is pure romantic love, unchecked by reason, a distortion of real love. Just as the play makes people laugh instead of crying, romantic love separates people instead of joining them, and destroys meaning instead of making life meaningful. Real love gets through to its object, or rather it is itself an exchange between two separate beings that joins them into one. Before they fall out, Hermia and Lysander enjoy this mutual love; they are considerate and see love as sympathy that makes for understanding:

> *Love takes the meaning in love's conference*
> (Act II, Scene ii, line 46)

True love is neither impossibly exalted nor animalistic; it sees the beloved tenderly but sanely, in terms of the ordinary necessaries of life:

> *But, like a sickness, did I loathe this food;*
> *But, as in health, come to my natural taste,*
> *Now I do wish it, love it, long for it,*
> *And will for evermore be true to it.*
> (Act IV, Scene i, lines 173-76)

And this real effective love doesn't cut the lovers off from the world, because it's creative, it makes something outside itself that can be fed back into the world again. In marriage, children are born. In the state, wise and sympathetic government results from the love between Theseus and Hippolyta. And, in the natural world, the love between Oberon and Titania generates an animating and ordering power in nature, heals people in trouble, and blesses human lovers with constancy, fertility, and peace.

Imagination, which seems to lie at the roots of both acting and poetry, and love also, looks two ways. As fantasy it is, as Theseus condemns it for being, barren wish-fulfilment, of which the most extreme example is madness. But it is also the sympathy which enables Theseus to see into the motives of the actors and forgive their foolishness. And – though Theseus doesn't think this matters – it's the creative power in art.

In *MND* the lovers run away from repression, and the actors from interference, to the wood, where, because of the fairy rulers' quarrel, all rules have gone by the board. Order in nature is broken, Puck is allowed to indulge his disruptive energies unrestrained, and lovers, actors, and Fairy Queen alike are overtaken by a kind of comic justice. Through enchantment, the dominant peculiarities of each are taken to their logical extremes. Bottom becomes an ass, Titania loves him, the lovers lose all contact with outside reality.

It's only when these extremes have been acted out, and the lovers at any rate have gone through a kind of death, that the miracle happens and the forces of destruction are converted to creative energies, at the moment, just before dawn, that Oberon and Titania are reconciled. Titania regains her wits, and Oberon the 'king of shadows,' gets back his wife. It is from their restored harmony that healing flows to the sleeping human beings:

> *Come, my Queen, take hands with me,*
> *And rock the ground whereon these sleepers be*
> (Act IV, Scene i, lines 85-6)

Now all the play's opposites begin to join. With morning Theseus and Hippolyta come to the wood, and that night Oberon and Titania visit the city. Reason, imagination, and passion combine in the marriages of both pairs of royal lovers; sympathy puts law in its place, energy obeys order.

In Acts IV and V there are moments of imaginative thickening, when contradictory kinds of experience unite. Theseus' and Hippolyta's discussion of their hounds' music becomes an image, like the fairy dance, for seemingly wild energy that's based on order (like the tremendous clamour of church bells rung with mathematical precision). It is, of course, an image of creative energy and love, both in the universe and between human beings.

> *I never heard*
> *So musical a discord, such sweet thunder*
> (Act IV, Scene i, lines 117-18)

Now love can do as it likes without any danger, and the lovers' new security is such that most of Act V, which celebrates their wedding, can be given up to a comic parody of the confusion, danger, silliness and disorder of their own past proceedings. And at the very end of the play, Puck brings the night, with all its fears, into the peaceful house, and the sense of mysterious darkness outside the protective walls adds to the excitement of satisfied love.

Many love-stories end a little flatly, with an after-taste of disappointment. But in *MND*, just as the lovers discover there are powers outside themselves that they can't penetrate, and that truth can be bigger than human understanding, so the fairies, night, and dreams will go on calling us, like death itself, away from ordinary life and security. And Puck's last words (Act V, Scene i, lines 411-15) are still more disturbing, as under the form of polite apology he suggests that life itself perhaps may be a dream,

> . . . *That you have but slumber'd here*
> *While these visions did appear.*
> *And this weak and idle theme,*
> *No more yielding but a dream,*
> *Gentles, do not reprehend.*

THEME INDEX

A **Midsummer Night's Dream** is about love and its cul-
mination in marriage. Acting is its second main theme.
There follows a selection of references to these themes and
related ones.

Love: I i 16-17, 26-38, 132-55, 181-201, 204-7, 226-51; II i
20-31, 60-117, 155-72, 188-244; II ii 46, 115-22; III ii 90-3,
114-15, 122-334, 440-1, 458-63; IV i 160-176; V i 1-11, 126-
348, 357-408.
The love-juice is more than a piece of plot machinery, for
its workings suggest what passion does to people—twisting
clear, reasonable sight and making its victims act as if in a
dream: II i 146-87, 245-68; II ii 27-34, 66-83, 102-44; III i
119-31; III ii 1-40, 88-121, 136-7, 345-77, 448-63; IV i 46-79.

Hate, love's opposite, is also love's twin. Sexual emotion is
extreme and violent, and the lovers must hate if they don't
love: I i 198-9; II i 211-12, 258; II ii 137-42; III ii 80, 149-54,
189-90, 227-8, 263-4, 269-70, 271-2, 280-1, 432-4; IV i 49,
63, 78-9, 142-5, 173.

Death, which hate can cause, is closely linked with love, and
also with night, sleep and tragedy. Love and joy are finally
powerful in *A Midsummer Night's Dream* because they
conquer death, disorder and darkness: I i 42-4, 65, 76-9,
86-7, 117-21, 141-9, 173-4; I ii 11-12, 20; II i 9-10, 18, 135,
189-90, 243-4; II ii 84, 101, 156; III i 9-18; III ii 47-9, 51-5,
56-80, 243-4, 269, 313, 364-5, 373, 381-7; IV i 217-18; V i
66-7, 143-8, 272-300, 312-39, 343-6, 361-8.

Barrenness is on the side of death; but in the play **fertility**
is stronger than barrenness, and **marriage** triumphs over
chastity (always lonely and at worst sheer waste): I i 1-19,
20-127, 156-63; I ii 5-7; II i 18-31, 60-145, 155-64; III ii 13,
35-77, 370-1; IV i 71-4, 87-92, 151-9, 179-81; IV ii 14-15;
V i 30-4, 349-56, 387-408.

Music and Dancing, like marriage itself, are images of concord and love, and of union between the play's opposing
forces, wood and city, imagination and reason, energy and
order: I i 30-1, 183-5, 189; II i 64-8, 82-90, 140-1, 148-54,
253-4; II ii 1, 7, 9-24; III i 98-103, 113-28; III ii 203-8; IV i
28-30, 81-3, 85-92, 106, 109-18, 123-7, 138, 143, 215-18; V i
32-4, 40-1, 60, 122-3, 340-1, 347-8, 377-86.

Acting comes second only to love in *A Midsummer Night's
Dream.* The wedding celebrations end in a play which unintentionally (on the part of the players) 'sends up' both
noble love and dramatic poetry. Laughter blots out love's
serious dangers, and **comedy and tragedy** become confused:
I i 11-19; I ii 1-104; II i 18, 44-57, 64-8, 87, 128-34, 141;
III i 1-109; III ii 5, 6-34, 114-15, 118-19, 122-344 (the lovers'
quarrel is a 'play' to Puck, and the lovers themselves think
the others are acting—Helena especially is convinced that
everything the others say is 'counterfeit'), 352-3, 360-5, 396-
430 (Puck imitates the two men, i.e. he acts their parts);
IV i 200-1, 215-18; IV ii 1-42; V i 56-70, 208-13, 344-7,
409-24.

There are, of course, other subsidiary themes, many of
them demonstrating the contrasts and contradictions at the
heart of the play: day/night; city/wood; sleep/waking;
reason/imagination; truth/falsehood; human beings/mon-
sters. These will no doubt all influence your understanding
and appreciation of the play as you study it.

FURTHER READING

The best introduction to *A Midsummer Night's Dream* is Chaucer's *The Knight's Tale.* Here Shakespeare found the Athenian setting, the identical lovers, and Theseus the wise ruler and judge – found also the conflict between civilization and deeper disorder, the city, and the wood where Palamon and Arcite fight up to the ankles in their own fresh blood. Chaucer's poem is darker, more massive and limited, embracing fewer possibilities than Shakespeare's play. In it the old gods, not the fairies, intervene, tragedy strikes, and human littleness is treated with serious irony. But romantic love in both works is at once intense and comic, both end in marriage and harmony, and in both an unusually clear and orderly construction masks a certain wonder at the strange contradictions of life.

You should go on to read Shakespeare's other comedies, particularly *Love's Labour's Lost, As You Like It* and *Romeo and Juliet*; the *Sonnets,* particularly 1–17, in which he tries to persuade a friend to marry (fruitfulness wars against the *barren rage of death's eternal cold* in 13); the last plays, particularly *The Tempest,* where the conditions of *A Midsummer Night's Dream* are reproduced but love and life itself fade away to nothing, like a pageant of a dream.

C. L. Barber's *Shakespeare's Festive Comedies* and J. R. Brown's *Shakespeare and his Comedies* are both excellent general studies, and Jan Kott's *Shakespeare our Contemporary,* is exciting though perverse. There are useful and interesting sections on the play, from various points of view, in Alexander Leggatt's *Shakespeare's Comedy of Love,* G. K. Hunter's *Shakespeare: Late Comedies* and Nevill Coghill's *Shakespeare's Professional Skills.* A clear, brief study of the play is Stephen Fender's *Shakespeare's A Midsummer Night's Dream.*

Good criticism yields useful information and helps to make you think, but in the end nothing can be as valuable as your own insight and interest in the play itself.